Jane Austen's Achievement

Also by Juliet McMaster
THACKERAY: THE MAJOR NOVELS

Jane Austen Bicentennial Conference, University of Alberta, 1975.

Jane Austen's Achievement

Papers delivered at the Jane Austen Bicentennial Conference at the University of Alberta

Edited by
JULIET McMASTER

DALE H. GRAMLEY LIBRARY
SALEM COLLEGE
WINSTON-SALEM, N. C.

BARNES & NOBLE

BOOKS
10 East 53d St., New York 10022
(a division of Harper & Row Publishers, Inc.)

PR
4037
J315
1975

© The Macmillan Press Ltd 1976
with the exception of Chapter 5 which is © Barbara Hardy 1975
All rights reserved. No part of this publication may be
reproduced or transmitted, in any form or by any means,
without permission

First published 1976 by
THE MACMILLAN PRESS LTD
London and Basingstoke

Published in the U.S.A. 1976 by
HARPER & ROW PUBLISHERS, INC.
BARNES & NOBLE IMPORT DIVISION

Library of Congress Cataloging in Publication Data

Jane Austen Bicentennial Conference, University of
    Alberta, 1975.
    Jane Austen's achievement.

    Includes bibliographical references and index.
    1.   Austen, Jane, 1775–1817—Criticism and interpre-
tation—Congresses. I. McMaster, Juliet. II. Title.
PR4037.J315   1975   823'.7   76–28821
ISBN 0–06–494734–3

Printed in Great Britain

Contents

Contents

Acknowledgements

The Edmonton conference which brought these speakers together was a delightful as well as a distinguished occasion, but now, regrettably, it is a past one. Those who were there will remember that the one shadow over the conference was the absence of Lionel Trilling, who had then just gone into hospital. His paper was to have been on 'Why we read Jane Austen' – and there is no one who would have been more fit to tell us about ourselves as well as the author we were gathered to celebrate. We did not know then how much we were losing: a month later we heard the news of his death.

I would like here to express my gratitude to the funding institutions which made possible the conference, and hence this collection: to the University of Alberta, the Canada Council, the British Council and the United States Embassy. I also want to thank Ian Jack, for coming at short notice to deliver a delightful paper (unfortunately not available for this collection); my colleagues, David Jackel, Noel Parker-Jervis, Norman Page and John Lauber, for their help in the organisation of the conference; and Brahma Chaudhuri, for editorial assistance.

Juliet McMaster

Contributors

LLOYD W. BROWN has taught in both Canada and the United States, and is now Professor of Comparative Literature at the University of Southern California, Los Angeles. His publications include *Bits of Ivory: Narrative Techniques in Jane Austen's Fiction*, *The Black Writer in Africa and the Americas*, and a forthcoming study of West Indian poetry.

BARBARA HARDY is Chairman of the Department of English at Birkbeck College, University of London, and present occupant of its Chair of Literature. She is the author of *The Novels of George Eliot*, *The Appropriate Form*, *The Moral Art of Dickens*, *The Exposure of Luxury: Radical Themes in Thackeray*, *Tellers and Listeners: The Narrative Imagination*, *A Reading of Jane Austen*, and the editor of *Middlemarch: Critical Approaches to the Novel* and *Critical Essays on George Eliot*.

A. WALTON LITZ is Professor of English and Chairman of the English Department at Princeton University. He is the author of *The Art of James Joyce*, *Jane Austen: A Study of Her Artistic Development*, *James Joyce* and *Introspective Voyager: The Poetic Development of Wallace Stevens*. He has also edited texts by Jane Austen and Thomas Hardy, and collections of essays on T. S. Eliot and modern American fiction. His most recent volume is an edition of *Major American Short Stories*.

JULIET MCMASTER took her first degree at St Anne's College, Oxford, and her graduate degrees at the University of Alberta, where she is now a Professor of English. She is the author of *Thackeray: The Major Novels*, and of a number of articles on Sterne, Jane Austen, Trollope, James, and others. She is currently working on a study of Trollope's Palliser novels, with the support of a Guggenheim fellowship.

NORMAN PAGE was educated at Emmanuel College, Cambridge, and

Leeds University. He is a Professor of English at the University of Alberta, and is the author of *The Language of Jane Austen, Speech in the Novel* and many articles on the novel, and editor of *Wilkie Collins: the Critical Heritage*. He has in preparation a book on Hardy and an edition of *Jude the Obscure*.

B. C. SOUTHAM, formerly a lecturer at Westfield College of the University of London, has more recently been Editorial Director at Routledge & Kegan Paul, and is now with Basil Blackwell Publisher. He is the author of books on Jane Austen, Tennyson and T. S. Eliot. His particular interest is in the relation between the writer and his times; and, in the case of Jane Austen, in understanding the contemporary Regency meanings of her words and references, and the novels' social and intellectual terms of reference.

GEORGE WHALLEY, Professor of English in Queen's University, was elected Rhodes Scholar in 1936, served with the Royal Navy during the war, and is a Fellow of the Royal Society of Canada. Author of *Poetic Process, Coleridge and Sara Hutchinson, The Legend of John Hornby*, and of a number of poems, essays, articles, and broadcasts, he is at present editing Coleridge's Marginalia for the *Collected Works of Samuel Taylor Coleridge*.

Abbreviations

E	*Emma*
Letters	*Jane Austen's Letters to her Sister Cassandra and Others*
MP	*Mansfield Park*
NA	*Northanger Abbey*
P	*Persuasion*
P&P	*Pride and Prejudice*
S	*Sanditon*
S&S	*Sense and Sensibility*
VI	*Minor Works*

References to Jane Austen's works are to R. W. Chapman's editions:
The Novels of Jane Austen, ed. R. W. Chapman, 5 vols, 3rd ed. (London: Oxford University Press, 1932–4)
Minor Works, ed. R. W. Chapman (London: Oxford University Press, 1954)
Jane Austen's Letters to her Sister Cassandra and Others, ed. R. W. Chapman, 2nd ed. (London: Oxford University Press, 1952)

There seems almost a general wish of decrying the capacity and undervaluing the labour of the novelist, and of slighting the performances which have only genius, wit, and taste to recommend them.

(Northanger Abbey, p. 37)

Today Jane Austen's playful complaint about the low critical status of her chosen medium has become superfluous, at least so far as her own novels are concerned. The following essays, written to celebrate the bicentenary of her birth, do full justice to her as a writer of keen intellect, significant vision, and impeccable artistry. Her genius, wit, and taste – as well as her irony that prompted the insertion of that 'only' – are here acknowledged.

Introduction

In a letter of 1974 to the *Times Literary Supplement*, Frank Brad-
brook humorously objected to the incongruity of the celebrations
planned for the bicentenary of Jane Austen's birth, which were
dotted all over the calendar, instead of concurring on the properly
accurate date of 16 December, her birthday.[1] She herself took pains
to get such things right, and so perhaps should her critics and
admirers. In his recent book Stuart Tave too enlarges on Jane
Austen's enjoyment and ability, in the novel as in the dance, 'in
moving with significant grace in good time in a restricted space'.[2]
It is the silly and dangerous characters in her fiction, he shows, like
the Thorpes and the Crawfords, who misrepresent and manipulate
time and space.

To celebrate the two-hundredth anniversary of Jane Austen's birth
in October, in Western Canada, is no doubt to be guilty of a comic
incongruity. But as though to compensate for the misdemeanour,
the papers delivered at the conference have a common and exact
focus on period and locale.

Though they are discrete studies and written independently, these
essays touch and expand on each other at many points. Local
habitations recurrently become centres of interest, and the description of Pemberley, which is so important a co-relative of Darcy's
identity, is echoed, quite unpremeditatedly, from one paper to
another: for Barbara Hardy Pemberley is the defining space which
provides Elizabeth with an accurate image of Darcy; Walton Litz
examines it as a manifestation of permanence, an example of Jane
Austen's early sense of the stability of self that was to give way to
a vision of a more fluid identity, as suggested by Anne Elliot's eventual commitment to a homeless sailor. And B. C. Southam finds in it
the achieved harmony between man and nature that needs no
'improvement', a space that time need no further modify.

'Improvement', a resonant term in Jane Austen criticism since
Alistair Duckworth's book, *The Improvement of the Estate*,[3] is

another concept that recurs from one paper to another, and it is investigated most fully by B. C. Southam in his wide-ranging examination of *Sanditon*. I have chosen to place his paper first in this collection, despite the apparent inappropriateness of beginning with a treatment of the last novel, because in fact it beautifully connects *Sanditon* with *Northanger Abbey*, the end of Jane Austen's career with the beginning; and because it firmly and vividly locates her in her own time. He shows her to be a novelist of ideas, writing, in her last novel especially, a work that is as topically pointed and as intellectually structured as Swift's *Tale of a Tub* or Peacock's *Headlong Hall*.

Lloyd Brown too looks at Jane Austen in her own time, but on a more personal level, drawing on her private pronouncements in her letters as evidence for the interpretation of her public statements in the novels. Like George Whalley, he takes issue with the standard view of Jane Austen as a comic writer; for he finds in her view of marriage and motherhood a bleak moral outlook, and a poignant statement about the plight of woman.

Norman Page's paper advances our attention to the Victorian and modern periods, where Jane Austen remains immanent as an influence, the founder of the 'great tradition' of Leavis's phrase. He introduces too another presiding genius of the conference, Henry James, who makes his gracious appearance in several of the papers. Walton Litz identifies 'the twentieth century's penchant for comparing [Jane Austen's] art to Henry James's'; and perhaps it is fitting that James too, after his benign condescension about 'our dear, everybody's dear, Jane', should be invoked, with all his critical prestige, to do belated justice to the wool-gathering spinster of his description.[4]

Walton Litz's paper, like Barbara Hardy's, utilises a quotation from James – the splendid discussion between Madame Merle and Isabel in *The Portrait of a Lady* on the nature of personal identity and its relation to surrounding objects – to throw light on a change in Jane Austen's view of the self as it developed through her career. 'What shall we call our "self"?' asks Madame Merle. Jane Austen's answer, Litz suggests, would have been different at the end of her career from what it was at the beginning. Madame Merle's answer is suggestive for Jane Austen too: 'It overflows into everything that belongs to us – and then it flows back again.'

Barbara Hardy's focus is on that 'everything that belongs to us', the 'properties and possessions' in the novels that are such important extensions of their owners, the characters. Her emphasis is spatial, on the being in space rather than the becoming in time, so that her paper and Litz's interestingly complement each other. Her exact and exacting scrutiny of the significant things in the novels – the objects treasured or neglected, the gifts generous or niggardly, the enclosing rooms and spaces that are the shells which organically express their inmates – is testimony that Jane Austen possessed and marvellously refined on that great virtue which James required of the novelist, specificity.

With the engaging modesty of a Coleridgean among Janeites, George Whalley nevertheless advances criticism of Jane Austen by a large stride. As Litz comments, Jane Austen had already been aligned with Aristotle and the *Poetics* by some of her nineteenth-century critics; but no one has so lucidly pursued that question of her 'poetry' that was so hotly in dispute between Charlotte Brontë and Lewes. If, as he fears, George Whalley is indeed sickening for a book on Jane Austen, his malady may be cheerfully anticipated by Austen scholars.

'Jane Austen, *poet*?' is one's initial doubtful reaction; but then, somehow, the proposition becomes acceptable and even familiar. After all, we always knew it. The fact that she wrote in prose is of course neither here nor there – Sidney dealt with that objection long ago when he announced 'there have been many most excellent Poets that never versified, and now swarme many versifiers that neede never aunswere to the name of Poets.' *Pride and Prejudice* manages to be 'light, and bright, and sparkling' because of qualities of timing and rhythm that belong to poetry. Walton Litz uses lines from Wallace Stevens to describe Jane Austen: 'there never was a world for her/Except the one she sang and, singing, made.' Stuart Tave's image of her as dancer, and his demonstration of the concentrated significance that is resident in her very words, are further testimony to our movement towards the appreciation not only of Jane Austen, novelist, but of Jane Austen, poet.

NOTES
1 18 Oct 1974, p. 1164.
2 *Some Words of Jane Austen* (Chicago and London, 1973) p. 1.
3 (Baltimore and London, 1971).
4 'The Lesson of Balzac', *The Atlantic Monthly*, xcvi (Aug 1905) pp. 167–8.

1 *Sanditon:* the Seventh Novel

B. C. SOUTHAM

Sanditon does not feature prominently in the criticism of Jane Austen and many studies happily ignore it altogether or merely mention it in passing as a biographical curiosity of small literary interest. The focus of attention is properly on the six completed novels. There is a limit to what can be said about a fragment only eleven and a half chapters long, a manuscript whose status is anyway questionable. While some critics believe that the text is reasonably close to the form in which it would one day have been sent to the printer (needing only paragraphing, the expansion of abbreviations and other trivial tidying-up), others view it as a rough draft, not a document upon which to base confident critical judgement.[1] The prevailing attitude towards *Sanditon* owes a good deal to E. M. Forster's influential review of the first edition in 1925;[2] up to this time, the fragment had been known only sketchily from the extracts given in the 1871 Memoir. Forster wrote with enthusiasm and some perception. He was a self-confessed Janeite and he came to *Sanditon* with the special understanding of a novelist who in his own style of comedy had learned much from Jane Austen's example. He was quick to recognise the new topographical rootedness of *Sanditon*. No one has identified this more succinctly and persuasively: 'not only does the sea dance in freshness, but another configuration has been given to the earth, making it at once more poetic and more definite'. But overall Forster was disappointed. He read the fragment diagnostically. He detected the author's bodily exhaustion in the exhaustion of the writing, the product of a failing imagination: the manuscript revisions 'are never in the direction of vitality'; the character-drawing is wholly in the grip of the earlier novels; and it 'gives the effect of weakness, if only because it is reminiscent from first to last.' These remarks are deceptively credible. At the end of January 1817, when she began *Sanditon*, Jane Austen was far into her last illness. Two months later, at the end of March, she abandoned the manuscript, unable to continue, and four months later she died.

Sanditon has been plagued by Forster's biographicalism. Much of the subsequent comment and criticism has lingered sentimentally on the circumstances of its composition and has stepped back in wonder at Jane Austen's creative resilience in embarking on a fierce satire of hypochondria and invalidism at such a dire moment in her own life. The biographical approach offers an appreciative tribute to Jane Austen's courage, detachment and wry humour in this enterprise. This does full justice to Jane Austen's human qualities; but it does less than justice to the literary qualities of *Sanditon* itself, which, in these terms, has commonly been treated as an outsider, a latecomer, pathetically stranded on the outskirts of the *oeuvre*. The curious and touching context of its writing has tended to distract attention from another, more important context, not the author's state of health at this time but *Sanditon*'s working relationship to the other novels. One aspect of this relationship has been explored in Marvin Mudrick's analysis of Jane Austen's irony, where *Sanditon* has the crowning place. It marks the 'Liberation of Irony' (as the last chapter is called), and the book ends on a very challenging note: 'To such works as *Emma* and *Persuasion*, *Sanditon* may – if only in its brevity and incompleteness – seem an epilogue; but it makes its own path. It is a new work; in the midst of her last illness, three months before her death at the age of forty-one, Jane Austen was undertaking with fresh impulse another liberation.'[3]

Professor Mudrick's account asks us to regard *Sanditon* as the beginning to a genuine seventh novel and to understand its strange and sometimes un-Austen-like features not as the deficiencies of a rough draft, nor, *vide* Forster, as ailing throwbacks to her earlier work, but as features of a new imaginative conception. The same case can be made for *Sanditon* when we look at it alongside the other late novels, in particular, alongside *Northanger Abbey* (which Jane Austen was revising in 1816, probably in the interval of five months following the completion of *Persuasion* in August and the beginning of *Sanditon*). Put in this context, *Sanditon* no longer looks like an oddity, an afterthought or a private joke for the family; and the chronological perspective brings out Jane Austen's attention to the concept of 'Improvement', a term prominent in the later novels, which touches upon some of the most important social and cultural debates of Regency England.[4] The 'Improvement' theme carries from *Mansfield Park* onwards to *Sanditon*, a progression that resists the usual assumption that Jane Austen's development ends in the autumnalism of *Persuasion* and that together the six novels compose the most compact and self-contained *oeuvre* in English literature. This is a fond illusion, a theory of cyclical evolution, in which *Persuasion* features as the older woman's mature and wise return to the theme of romantic love so caustically treated by the younger woman in *Sense and Sensibility*. *Sanditon* upsets the evolutionary view; and the 'Improvement' theme calls up a slightly unusual Jane Austen − a writer historically conscious, who regarded herself, in part, as an historian of social change in a period of extreme change, and in whose later works there is an increasingly important dimension of contemporary reference, so much so that the novels are distinctly *contemporary* novels which provide a descriptive and analytical commentary on Regency society and its values. This is not to disregard the novels' timeless qualities as works of art portraying the unchanging elements of human nature, but to draw attention to their historical significance, an aspect of their meaning which is often ignored.

The question of contemporary reference faced Jane Austen very sharply when she came to revise *Northanger Abbey* in 1816. The manuscript of this early novel (written about 1798−9) had been out of her hands since 1803, when it was sold to the publisher Crosby and remained with him, unpublished − probably because he thought that the Gothic satire market was over-crowded − until Henry Austen bought it back in 1816.

Although nothing has survived to show us the exact nature of the changes made at this time, we can be fairly certain that as far as the style was concerned, the 1816 revision was very thorough indeed. For while *Northanger Abbey* is structurally, and in its characterisation, the simplest and least developed of the novels, it is also the most flawless. Its writing is quite free from the unevenness and stiffness that crop up occasionally in the other two early novels. Its comic tone is remarkably assured and the sustained brilliance of the writing can only be the fruits of this late revision. But Jane Austen made no attempt to bring the story and background up to date. This is Bath of the late 1790s, with the manners and types of the period. There is one literary reference as late as 1801. Otherwise, the novel is set a year or so earlier, at the height of the Gothic fashion. While Jane Austen could feel confident of its success as a piece of entertainment, she was anxious to warn the public that unlike her other late novels, this one was not contemporary and she supplied an 'Advertisement' to this effect, summarising the book's checkered history: that it had gone for publication in 1803, that 'thirteen years have passed since it was finished, and many more since it was begun, and that during that period, places, manners, books, and opinions have undergone considerable changes.' One obvious anxiety would be the Gothic satire. Although in 1816 *Udolpho* was still well known and currently in print, the literary joke had inevitably lost some of its point. In particular, coming fresh from *Persuasion*, which is set in the post-war years of 1814–15, Jane Austen would have been thinking about the considerable changes in the social structure of Bath.

Bath of the 1790s had been a social mixing-pot. Everyone jostled together in the Public Rooms of the Spa. This is how such a non-entity as a Catherine Morland, the daughter of an obscure country clergyman, can bump into a Henry Tilney, the son of a great land-owner; and how they in turn can meet the Thorpes, the children of a rising lawyer. But over the next ten or fifteen years Bath changed. It became less fashionable, less popular with the gentry, less of a marriage-market for their children. It was gradually taken over by the lower middle classes, people we hear so much about in *Emma* – the ambitious farmers of the west country, the merchants of Bristol, the manufacturers of Birmingham, the lawyers and medical men. These were the social groups which benefited most from the prosperity of the Napoleonic wars. They were not born into the ranks of the gentry. But they wanted to share the gentry's social standing, as far as that could be achieved, by mixing with them, by imitating their style of life, their manners and their speech. The older gentry continued to come to Bath from season to season out of habit, to meet up with their friends again and because they disliked the brashness and informality of the new watering-places along the coast. They turned their backs on this new generation of visitors and kept to themselves. This is the post-war Bath of *Persuasion*, of the Elliots and their ageing cronies. There, Catherine Morland and Henry Tilney would never have met. The gentry had abandoned the Public Rooms to the *hoi polloi*. They kept to their own circles, entertaining in private, and were able to maintain their snobbish rituals in observing the fine gradations of rank between the lesser and the greater gentry. In such a closed society a Tilney would pass his time in one set, a Morland in another, and their paths would not have crossed. Anne Elliot is nearly trapped with this same problem.

She is worried about her chances of meeting Wentworth at Bath and Jane Austen is at pains to lay out the precise and prosaic social detail of the situation: 'The theatre or the rooms, where he was most likely to be, were not fashionable enough for the Elliots, whose evening amusements were solely in the elegant stupidity of private parties . . .' (p. 180).

As a supreme artist in the comedy of manners, Jane Austen prided herself on this degree of precision and accuracy in social observation. So the *Northanger Abbey* 'Advertisement' can be read as a careful step to protect her reputation for period fidelity. It was a quality which the reviewers had already remarked upon in the earlier novels and she felt it important to explain to her public, an audience very close to her, why this latest story was rather dated. But Jane Austen's concern went further than this. The changes in the pattern of Bath society were not simply local and superficial; they were part of a wider and deeper pattern of change running throughout English society. The forty years of Jane Austen's lifetime was a period of transition. The Georgian world of the eighteenth century, 'the old society' as it was known, was being carried, uneasily and reluctantly, into the early nineteenth-century world of the Regency, into a self-consciously 'new' society, boasting of its modern outlook and modern values, and turning its back upon many of the traditions of the past. This process of change came in the wake of the Industrial Revolution; and during the years Jane Austen was writing, it gained fresh impetus from the economic boom that Britain enjoyed as a manufacturing and trading nation during the Napoleonic wars.

Contemporary historians and commentators identified this process, optimistically and flatteringly, as a process of *Improvement*. They described their age as The Age of Improvement, as it was, indisputably, in material wealth, supporting a middle-class gentry rich and leisured enough to turn Improvement into a way of life – with improved manners, improved fashions, improved morality, education, accomplishments and so on. It becomes a key word in cultural and scientific literature, displayed in the titles of books and articles, and it defined for its users what they confidently regarded as the distinctive feature of the Regency Enlightenment. The most conspicuous improvement was across the face of the countryside itself, in the utilitarian and functional change effected by the agricultural revolution, which brought in scientific farming and saw the enclosure and cultivation of waste land and commons, a process of land utilisation which was greatly accelerated by the fear that a Napoleonic sea blockade would force the country to be agriculturally self-sufficient. The other conspicuous countryside improvement was the Reptonian improvement of great houses and their grounds, as General Tilney's 'improving hand' has transformed the pre-reformation convent of Northanger Abbey into a modern home of ostentatious and ingenious luxury, and as Henry Crawford spins his inventive mind around the improvement of Sotherton Court and Thornton Lacey. At its best, landscape improvement could achieve subtle and magnificent effects, as Elizabeth Bennet observes from the windows of Pemberley House. But there was a darker side too. For the radicals of the age, improvement was a cant word, a symbol of Regency pride, pretentiousness and showy wealth. They spat it out as a term of abuse and Cobbett never tires of pointing to the estates where the wonders of improvement had cost the destruction of farms and villages and the beggaring of their inhabitants.

Jane Austen is the most important nineteenth-century historian of 'Improvement' and of the process of change that it signified; and 'Improvement' would make an apt thematic title for *Mansfield Park*, where an elaborate sematic drama is formed around the whole concept of improvement, exploiting its landscape associations, playing with its technical vocabulary, and carrying these ideas into the mental and moral landscapes of the characters. One of Mary Crawford's slyest remarks, intended to upset Fanny Price and to intrigue Edmund with her spirit and daring, is the comment with which she crowns Mrs Rushworth's account of Sotherton chapel and her late husband's abandonment of family prayers: 'Every generation has its improvements' (p. 86), (a remark which reminds us of her previous 'improvement' joke about 'improvements *in hand* as the greatest of nuisances' [p. 57], another suggestive pun about her uncle's behaviour). Part of Jane Austen's purpose in the novel is to explore how diverse, often contradictory, the interpretation of 'improvement' could be, not just between the old generation and the new but also between the different moral and cultural worlds that are represented by the Crawfords, the Bertrams and Fanny Price.

These ideas were very close to Jane Austen when she was working on *Northanger Abbey* in 1816, both in the 'improvement' comedy around General Tilney, and in *Persuasion*, the manuscript which she had just finished. Improvement in social status qualifies a humble Wentworth to ask for the hand of an Elliot. Eight years earlier, he had been unacceptable to Lady Russell and the baronet. But the years of victory had brought the navy prize money and a heroic standing. Sir Walter now has to accept Wentworth's social and financial fitness. The landowner is bankrupt. A new social order, born of the war, has come into being, and he is forced to receive an Admiral into his family home and a mere Captain into the family itself. At a more humble level the Musgroves, too, are caught up in this process of change. 'The Musgroves, like their houses, were in a state of alteration, perhaps of improvement. The father and mother were in the old English style, and the young people in the new. Mr. and Mrs. Musgrove were a very good sort of people; friendly and hospitable, not much educated, and not at all elegant. Their children had more modern minds and manners' (p. 40). The Musgrove family portrait in 'the old-fashioned square parlour' looks down in amazement as it sees the room gradually being given 'the proper air of confusion by a grand piano forte and a harp, flower-stands and little tables placed in every direction' by the 'daughters of the house' (p. 40). This triumph of tasteful 'confusion' over the old-fashioned 'neatness' and order, is a mild domestic image, playfully delivered. But the lightness of the tone here doesn't take away from the force of Jane Austen's quasi-historical definition of 'the old English style' and the 'new', of the 'old' manners and the 'more modern minds and manners' of the next generation. Jane Austen's own attitude – of quiet amusement, and behind that, a judgement suspended and withheld – is conveyed by the hesitation in her choice of words, 'alteration, perhaps . . . improvement'.

The *Persuasion–Northanger Abbey* context bears closely upon *Sanditon*. Having just brought *Northanger Abbey* up to date stylistically, it is as if, in *Sanditon*, Jane Austen is bringing *Northanger Abbey* up to date historically, giving its satire an immediate contemporary point and developing the work with one eye upon what she had described in *Persuasion* as the 'new' style in English society, what Mr Elliot calls disdainfully 'the unfeudal tone of the present day' (p. 139), with its 'modern' mind and modern manners and its ambivalent hesitation between 'alteration' and 'improvement'. *Sanditon* can be regarded as a recasting of *Northanger Abbey*. Jane Austen marks the connection jokingly by returning again to the archaic Fanny Burney device which she had employed to launch the earlier novel – getting the comedy of manners under way by tracing the experiences of an innocent and marriageable young woman on her first entry into society, with all the conventional pitfalls of fashionable behaviour and the embarrassments of dealing with unwelcome suitors. The burlesque parallels are intentional. Catherine Morland comes fresh from her Wiltshire village, the eldest daughter in a family of ten children, Charlotte Heywood from the remoteness of Willingden, the eldest daughter still at home out of fourteen children.

Sanditon repairs a slight clumsiness in the structure of *Northanger Abbey*, which, according to one theory, may have been first put together by joining two of the childhood pieces – a pastiche of the Fanny Burney situation and a Gothic satire – and running the two stories together, with a single heroine, using Bath as the stage for the parade of character types and the round of embarrassments and the Abbey as the setting for the Gothic reversal. In *Sanditon*, the two locations are combined. Bath's pre-eminence as fashionable middle-class gathering ground had by that time been lost to the coastal resorts which had also gained a reputation for rakishness. Sanditon is too young to have won Brighton's notoriety as a favoured spot for assignation and elopement. But it already has its statutory seducer, one of those wicked baronets that Mrs Morland was supposed to warn her daughter against, who 'delight in forcing young ladies away to some remote farm-house' (*NA*, p. 18). The joke is now modernised and pushed further. The baronet in *Sanditon* is too poor to indulge in the 'masterly style' of seduction in 'some solitary House' in 'the Neighbourhood of Tombuctoo' but is still ready to plot 'the quietest sort of ruin & disgrace' near at hand (pp. 405–6). The joke about Sir Edward is not just that he is re-markably adaptable; he is also slightly old-fashioned and out of touch with the geography of dissipation. He is still thinking of legendary Timbuctoo, fabled for its remoteness, its exotic pleasures and riches. But this romantic image had been shattered in the reports of Mungo Park and Robert Adams, which gave a disenchanted European view of Timbuctoo's alien and unpalatable native culture. These travellers' tales had only recently appeared – Mungo Park had been reprinted in 1815, Adams was published in 1816, and both books were extensively reviewed and quoted from in the monthlies and quarterlies. Imcompetent as a latter-day Lovelace, Sir Edward is also laughably out of date in his Regency Afro-Gothicism.

Sir Edward Denham is one of a range of complex character types set up for the heroine to encounter, to puzzle out and understand. The cast of eccentrics forms part of the peculiar social ethos of Sanditon, a place of wonder and novelty, which has to be observed and interpreted in much the same way that Catherine Morland has to try to digest the meaning of the Abbey as it really is, in broad daylight, and understand its owner in his real character. Both girls bring their preconceptions: Catherine, her Gothic fantasies; Charlotte, the scepticism inherited from her father and the country remoteness of Willingden. She is a strong-minded girl, in the 'old' style, with an un-modern mind and un-modern manners, finding herself set down in a strange and slightly dubious society. Instead of a Montoni or a General Tilney she is confronted by other varieties of neo-Gothicism in the complex enigma of Lady Denham, in the manifold absurdities of Sir Edward, and in the puzzles and contradictions that surround the other figures and form an atmosphere of mystery and uncertainty as dense as that Catherine Morland enters upon when she comes to stay with the Tilneys.

The revision of *Northanger Abbey* may also have led Jane Austen towards the idea of focusing closely upon a single place, describing it in detail and linking it with the enthusiasm of an improver. General Tilney and the Abbey are a convincing analogue. It is the most minutely and elaborately detailed of all Jane Austen's country-house locations, and provides a striking contrast to the insubstantiality of Bath in *Northanger Abbey*. Architecturally, Bath was one of the sights of Europe; 'it looks a city of palaces, a town of hills, and a hill of towns', was Fanny Burney's impression (jotted in her diary) in 1791.[5] But Jane Austen had no eye for the beauty and splendour of the town; for her purposes, it was merely a *social* location. However, as soon as the story reaches the Abbey, the location becomes significant. It enters into the imaginative experience of the novel with the defined structure and dimension of space that we find in Sanditon.

The Abbey's improver is an improver of the 1790s, a landowner extravagant in his wealth and fired with the 'genius' of invention, his kitchen his 'vanity', his garden his 'hobby-horse'. Mr Parker is a landowner of the next generation, a 'projector' on fire with the genius of commercial speculation. Significantly, Jane Austen uses the same word: his 'hobby-horse' is Sanditon. If Jane Austen had lived to complete the fragment, this repetition would have faced her readers as they moved from *Northanger Abbey*, the novel last published, to *Sanditon*, the latest, and this element of historical contrast would have been firmly before them.

In the earlier novels, Jane Austen had already put a question mark against the 'improvement' of places (as distinct from any other kind of improvement): quite simply, the moral places are *un*improved, or, if improved at all, unnoticeably so, and with great emphasis upon the hand of nature, as Elizabeth Bennet first sees Pemberley:

> a large, handsome, stone building ... in front, a stream of some natural importance was swelled into greater, but without any artificial appearance. Its banks were neither formal, nor falsely adorned. Elizabeth was delighted. She had never seen a place for which nature had done more, or where natural beauty had been so little counteracted by an awkward taste; ... and at that moment she felt, that to be mistress of Pemberley might be something! (*P&P*, p. 245)

When Emma Woodhouse surveys the familiar scene of Donwell Abbey, looking at it (towards the end of the novel) with a newly-awakened interest, she sees 'the respectable size and style of the building, its suitable, becoming, characteristic situation, ... with all the old neglect of prospect, ... its abundance of timber in rows and avenues, which neither fashion nor extravagance had rooted up ... It was just what it ought to be, and it looked what it was' (*E*, p. 358).

These places are naturally and unpretentiously themselves. Jane Austen's approval is carried in the simplicity and firmness of statement; in a style which is itself unelaborated and unimproved: Elizabeth's impression of what it might be 'to be mistress of Pemberley'; Emma's happy confirmation that Donwell Abbey 'was just what it ought to be, and ... looked what it was'. Here, as elsewhere in the novels, Jane Austen is playing with an emblematic interpretation of landscape, whereby a gentleman's character and social standing could be read in the appearance of his house and grounds. With the development of landscaping theory in the eighteenth century and its later sophistication into the philosophy of improvement, this basic idea became considerably elaborated, to the point that Repton was discovering 'the spirit of freedom and independence' in 'the heart-enlivening prospect' of 'the country residence of an English gentleman'. He set a social aim as the 'true end of all plans of improvement'. The landowners' objective should be 'to extend the dominion of elegance around their own habitations, and diffuse cheerfulness and comfort' among their dependents, to promote a benevolent relationship with their tenants and peasantry. Jane Austen sounds the chords of this theory, to raise an echo, and then passes beyond the theory to grasp the true substance of these places and their owners. Inside Pemberley and outside, in its grounds, Elizabeth discovers a congruence, a composed and extended image of strength, solidity and tradition, attaching to Darcy as a man of property and power properly used, a man capable of exerting authority, capable too of containing her and providing her with a refuge from the pressures and disorder of Longbourn. Donwell Abbey is the image of George Knightley's straightforward and unpretentious dignity, his transparent honesty; and a few pages later, Jane Austen celebrates the charming and disarming Englishness of this country scene, consorting so perfectly with what she describes as Knightley's 'true English style' (*E*, p. 99).

The counter-image to these places is drawn in Henry Crawford's proposals for an improved Thornton Lacey. 'From being the mere gentleman's residence, it becomes, by judicious improvement, the residence of a man of education, taste, modern manners, good connections. All this may be stamped on it; and that house receive such an air as to make its owner be set down as the great land-holder of the parish' (*MP*, p. 244). This is the emblematic theory parodied. The fitness of Pemberley and Donwell Abbey and the satisfaction they convey derive partly from the quality of their ownership, the accord between these men and the places they live in, and partly from the historical character of landscape that has been allowed to shape itself over centuries and carries a sense of respectful, uninterfering care. Henry Crawford's improvement is thin and theatrical, a mere façade, a character fabricated and imposed for the sake of effect. It is indeed to be emblematic: this is his notion of the proper public face for a country clergyman to show to the world, the declaration of faith, as it were, of a Rev. Henry Crawford; and it completes his sister's agreeable fantasies of being a vicar's wife in 'the respectable, elegant, modernized, and occasional residence of a man of independent fortune' (*MP*, p. 248).

In *Northanger Abbey* and *Sanditon*, Jane Austen enters more fully into the larger contemporary debate about the effect of improvement upon the English way of life and its impact as a cultural force. Was improvement the distinguishing character of a new and enlightened age, or a dangerous fad, a passing but destructive fashion, a threat to time-honoured values and traditions? *Northanger Abbey* poses this question in the context of the 1790s. One of the liveliest arguments of the time concerned the fate of old buildings, now that the Gothic taste, formerly a harmless and curious eccentricity, had blown up into a positive 'rage' for restoring and improving religious buildings and ruins, often converting them into spectacular and fashionable homes. Historians and antiquaries protested that this was not the

DALE H. GRAMLEY LIBRARY
SALEM COLLEGE
WINSTON-SALEM. N. C.

guardian spirit of 'preservation' but damaging theft by appropria-
tion. They complained that the 'Traits of our Ancient Magnificence'
were in more danger from restoration than from decay. In the shadow
of the French Revolution, these fears were given a patriotic edge:
in such dangerous times, with radicalism in the air, it seemed even
more important that the country should hold fast to its institutions
and preserve the visible heritage embodied in these monuments of
the past.

But amongst the Wyatts and the Reptons, the General Tilneys
and the Henry Crawfords – the practitioners and their clients –
restoration and improvement were regarded as a means of conferring
the benefits of modern taste. Improvement was an assertion of the
spirit and style of the new, 'unfeudal' society, with its distinctive
lightness, elegance, comfort, utility and cheerfulness – the modern
litany of landscaping and architecture. Improvement could be a
liberation: for Mr Rushworth, Sotherton is 'a prison – quite a dismal
old prison' (*MP*, p. 53), an Elizabethan house waiting for Repton's
cheerful hand to give it 'a modern dress' (p. 56). Sometimes there
was even a note of triumph at the occupation of religious buildings,
a heavy Anglican-Regency satisfaction at living opulently in places
once sacred to Catholicism. To call one's home an Abbey could be
to make a claim about the present age rather than to honour history.

The main lines of this debate enter amusingly into the comedy of
Catherine Morland's disillusionment. The Abbey is sufficiently
Gothic to feed her imagination. The General parades himself as a
man of culture. He speaks fervently of having preserved the 'Gothic
form' of the Abbey's windows with 'reverential care' (*NA*, p. 162),
even though the ancient glass has gone. He has maintained the
romantic appeal of its grounds and setting; and the formal rooms
have an appropriate spaciousness and grandeur unchanged from
previous generations.

The Abbey is also sufficiently anti-Gothic to make a fool of the
heroine. What strikes her first, on the night of her arrival, is its
modernity, not its antiquity. The drawing-room is furnished 'in all
the profusion and elegance of modern taste' and instead of an
ancient fire-place she sees the latest invention, a little patent
Rumford (p. 162). The modernised Abbey is an *anti*-Udolpho; and
the General, in his modish and determined pursuit of the latest
fashion, an *anti*-Montoni – a smooth and urbane Regency gentleman,
whose Abbey has been transformed into a home of domestic utility
and comfort.

The joke takes a further turn. Whilst the Abbey is an anti-Udolpho, it is also a *neo*-Udolpho; and the General a *neo*-Montoni. The domestication and modernising of the Abbey have been pushed to extremes. The improvements and innovations are elaborate to the point of fantasy. The conducted tour of the Abbey and its grounds leaves Catherine dizzied and overwhelmed. Inside and outside the house the sights are astounding: the kitchen-garden so huge, of such a number of acres as Catherine 'could not listen to without dismay, being more than double the extent of all Mr. Allen's, as well as her father's, including church-yard and orchard. The walls seemed countless in number, endless in length; a village of hot-houses seemed to arise among them, and a whole parish to be at work within the inclosure' (p. 178). Of course, Catherine is an innocent abroad, wide-eyed and wondering. In her fanciful imagination these impressions blossom fantastically. Yet the imagery is also allusive: the 'walls ... countless in number, endless in length', the 'village of hot-houses', the 'whole parish ... at work' follow the hyperbolism of Timon's villa:

> To compass this, his building is a town,
> His pond an ocean, his parterre a down.
> *(Moral Essays: Epistle IV*, ll. 105–6)

In a footnote, Pope explains that his description 'is intended to comprise the principles of a false taste of magnificence'. Jane Austen's purpose is equally specific. The shift is from an Augustan to a Regency Timon. The General's modern 'false taste of magnificence' has transformed the Abbey into a strange and whimsical showpiece. The Abbey has become a playground for the General's inventive genius and his appetite for display: outside, in the luxury of his 'pinery' and the elaboration of his 'succession-houses', his gardens 'unrivalled in the kingdom' (p. 178); inside, in the extraordinary and sacriligious modernisation of the convent kitchen, a description which Jane Austen delivers with a fulsome and resonant irony:

the ancient kitchen of the convent, rich in the massy walls and smoke of former days, and in the stoves and hot closets of the present. The General's improving hand had not loitered here: every modern invention to facilitate the labour of the cooks, had been adopted within this, their spacious theatre; and, when the genius of others had failed, his own had often produced the perfection wanted. His endowments of this spot alone might at any time have placed him high among the benefactors of the convent. (p. 183)

Beyond the kitchen, the fourth side of the Abbey is given over to the extensive and elaborately-equipped domestic offices, housing a multitude of servants. This, the General admits to Catherine, is his 'vanity ... in the arrangement of his offices'; and he unctuously pardons himself for showing her round this utilitarian part of the Abbey, 'as he was convinced, that, to a mind like Miss Morland's, a view of the accommodations and comforts, by which the labours of her inferiors were softened, must always be gratifying' (p. 184).

In this portrait of General Tilney Jane Austen's readers would have recognised the features of Rumford, the inventor of the General's smoke-free fireplace. Rumford was a real scientist. But he was also a standing joke of the age, lampooned and caricatured as a crackpot, a figure of inventive lunacy. He produced a great succession of ideas for gadgetry about the house, especially for the kitchen, (which one 'Rumfordised'), and he wrote about these inventions at staggering length. In his *Proposals for Establishing the Royal Institution* (1799), the long list of 'new mechanical inventions and improvements ... to the common purposes of life' includes all three of General Tilney's enthusiasms – the kitchen, kitchen equipment and hot-houses. In his gimmickry, his inventive genius run wild, his pursuit of domestic and mechanical improvement, General Tilney is Rumfordian man – a modern Timon caught up in the rage for novelty and the pride of conspicuous wealth. And in his pious concern for the welfare of his servants, Jane Austen may be sounding another Rumfordian note, since the inventor's schemes were usually produced with a great flourish of benevolent social philosophy, as transparently rhetorical as the General's sanctimonious little comment to Catherine, about 'the labours of her inferiors'. Some of Rumford's proposals were notorious – his recommendation of stale bread as a suitable diet for the poor, since 'it prolongs the duration of the enjoyment of eating';[6] his recommendation of soup-kitchens for the moral benefit to be gained from communal eating; his recipe for a poor-man's broth so rich in water that it was immediately christened Count Rumford's 'metaphysical soup'. Some of these suggestions smack of Swift's *Modest Proposal*; they were put forward in the late 1790s when the working population of England was living on the verge of starvation. Rumford prided himself as a philanthropist-thinker and there may be an echo of this activity in the rather mysterious remarks that General Tilney makes to Catherine on her second evening at the Abbey about having 'many pamphlets to finish' before he can go to bed 'and perhaps may be poring over the affairs of the nation for hours after you are asleep. Can either of us be more meetly employed? *My* eyes will be blinding for the good of others; and *yours* preparing by rest for future mischief' (p. 187). The General seems to be passing himself off as a man with a social conscience, another piece of fashionable humbug that could connect him with Rumford.

The Rumford joke was still current when Jane Austen returned to *Northanger Abbey* in 1816. He died only two years earlier and his memory lived on in the discussion of his scientific ideas, which were being reviewed more and more critically and which were of sufficient public interest to be extensively discussed in the quarterlies. During his lifetime, his books circulated very widely and were extremely popular for their combination of practical advice and high-minded philosophising. They were a source of amusement as well as of instruction. Smoking chimneys, for example, inspired him to a 'Philosophical Investigation'; a mundane topic, but in Rumford's system of thought 'connected with many of the most essential enjoyments of life' and thus vital 'to all those who feel pleasure in promoting or in contemplating the comfort and happiness of mankind'.[7] He was capable of dignifying household hints into reflections on the state of humanity and the condition of civilisation, delivered at enormous length. (*Essay X: On the construction of kitchen fireplaces* (1799) is 384 pages long.) In small doses, Rumford is a joy to read, very personal and quirky in style, and always faintly ridiculous for his earnestness and solemnity. His discourses on food, its preparation, cooking and eating go into the most exhaustive detail, down to the correct method for putting the spoon into the mouth, since, as he is careful to explain, 'the pleasure of eating, depends very much indeed upon the *manner* in which the food is applied to the organs of taste'.[8] Altogether, Rumford's writings in this area form a culinary prose epic, veering ludicrously between the sublime and the mundane, a grandiose discourse on the importance of food to the individual and to mankind – a kitchen equivalent to Erasmus Darwin's splendid systematic poems on botany and evolution, *The Botanic Garden* (1789, 1791) and *Zoonomia* (1794–6).

Jane Austen must have read Rumford with enjoyment. We hear his voice in the tea-time conversation between Sir Edward Denham and Charlotte Heywood, when he explains to her the dangers of dry toast to the 'Coats of the Stomach' and the protective powers of butter. But Sir Edward is baffled by the effect of green tea: 'The use of my right Side is entirely taken away for several hours!' Unimpressed, Charlotte advises him to have faith in science of the Rumford school: 'It sounds rather odd to be sure – ... but I dare say it would be proved to be the simplest thing in the World, by those who have studied right sides & Green Tea scientifically & thoroughly understand all the possibilities of their action on each other' (p. 418).[9] Charlotte gives this answer 'coolly'. It is really Jane Austen's answer to Rumford's inflated and optimistic philosophy, the belief that science, including what Rumford called 'mechanical improvement', was an index of the superiority of Regency civilisation. In his Royal Institution *Proposals* Rumford is insistent on 'the real importance' of 'improvement': 'that the pre-eminence of any people is, and ought ever to be, estimated by the state of *taste*, *industry*, and *mechanical improvement* among them' and he expresses his confidence that 'the inhabitants of this happy island, who have meditated profoundly on this interesting subject, will be very far indeed from being indifferent to the progress of improvement ... for they well know how powerfully the vivifying rays of Science, when properly directed, tend to excite the activity, and increase the energy, of an enlightened nation'. Jane Austen picks up Rumford with the touch of solemn ridicule. According to Charlotte Heywood, these are the 'rays' to solve the problems of Sir Edward's green-tea paralysis. These *mechanical improvements*, marking the pre-eminence of an 'enlightened nation', are the inventions with which General Tilney has endowed the convent kitchen.

While we can point to a close connection between *Sanditon* and *Northanger Abbey*, and following the theme of improvement, trace a pattern of continuity with the earlier novels, *Sanditon* is remarkable not for these associations but for the radical change it signifies in Jane Austen's art, away from the comedy of character and towards the comedy of ideas. The rich mental and emotional life of the heroines is missing from *Sanditon*, and there is no longer a focus upon the development of character and the exploration of relationships.

Charlotte Heywood is labelled as the heroine and occupies the heroine's role. She has the heroine's function, too, as Jane Austen's point of observation for much of the story. We can laugh at her jokes, enjoy her impressions of Sanditon, her delight at its bizarre inhabitants, her cool watchfulness and reserve, her primness when Sir Edward begins to warm excessively. However, these attitudes and responses compose a figure at a distance. There is no attempt to bring her within range of our affection or sympathy; no suggestion that she is going to be developed into a living personality as warm and attractive as Catherine Morland. Clara Brereton is held even further off and the rest of the cast are confined to comic roles in an unremitting satire of social and literary manners. The powerfully drawn gallery of eccentrics has an eighteenth-century flavour, with touches of Fielding, Smollett and Sterne. Yet such an extreme mode of artificial comedy, with characters so specifically typed and labelled in their literary and social roles, is unprecedented in Jane Austen and reminds us more of Sheridan and Congreve than of any eighteenth-century novelist.

Nevertheless, Jane Austen may also have been encouraged towards this new style of fiction by two very recent books, both published in 1815, Peacock's *Headlong Hall*, and *The Magic of Wealth* by Thomas Skinner Surr.

Headlong Hall was Peacock's first attempt at a discussion novel, where he brings together a group of opinionated and idiosyncratic characters to indulge their fanaticism on a wide range of contemporary topics. Amongst his targets were 'theorists in all sciences, projectors in all arts, morbid visionaries, romantic enthusiasts' and every variety of humbug and cant. The book opens with four 'illuminati' on board a coach beginning a lively discussion on 'improvements'. Mr Foster, 'the perfectibilian' declares that 'every thing we look on attests the progress of mankind in all the arts of life, and demonstrates their gradual advancement towards a state of unlimited perfection'; Mr Escot, 'the deteriorationist' regards these improvements as 'only so many links in the great chain of corruption'; while Mr Jenkinson, 'the statu-quo-ite' is content to find a state of perfect balance, neither progress nor decline. The fourth of the illiminati, the Rev. Dr Gaster, has only time to clear his throat and begin to complain at such 'a very sceptical' and 'atheistical conversation' when the coachman announces breakfast, and in his eagerness to get out, Dr Gaster twists his ankle. The coachman has an intrusive presence in this first chapter; and it looks very much as if Jane Austen is reminding us of *Headlong Hall* at the beginning of *Sanditon*, where in the opening sentences there is an otherwise puzzling focus upon the coachman, and then the injury to Mr Parker's ankle. These resemblances could well be Jane Austen's declaration that she was beginning her own style of discussion novel, with a similar contest of views between Mr Parker and Mr Heywood, the enthusiastic improver versus the sceptical and reactionary gentleman-farmer whose faith is in the sober stability of country life.

Peacock assembles his characters at Headlong Hall, Jane Austen at Sanditon, and in the vivid monologues of Mr Parker, Diana Parker and, most of all, Sir Edward Denham (who is a ventriloquial mouth-piece for a procession of topics – sentimentalism, melodramatic romanticism, potted science; and with the novel's continuation, doubtless there would be many more topics to follow), there is a satirical comedy-of-ideas pattern interwoven with the immediate social comedy of manners. Jane Austen's allusion to Peacock has the same purpose as the allusion to Fanny Burney in *Northanger Abbey*: not as a tribute, but as an invitation for the reader to see how much more skilful *her* performance is and to see how the novel can really be brought to answer its challenging definition as a 'work in which the greatest powers of the mind are displayed' (*NA*, p. 38). In Peacock the blatant *un*reality of the fiction is part of the joke. His literary devices are burlesque and caricature; and the plot and setting are simply a framework to give the characters somewhere to speak, to set them in motion and to bang their heads together. In *Sanditon*, Jane Austen's oblique comment is to the effect that the discussion novel, amusing enough in itself, does not really add up to very much as a work of art; for *that*, there has to be the reality of human experience, either in the characters themselves or through the author's perception and artistic presence within the novel. Peacock's deficiency is that he is only able to proceed by way of a drastic comic simplification; Jane Austen's artistry in *Sanditon* is to achieve the same comic effect, but without simplification, and within further patterns of meaning.

Like Peacock, Surr was also trying out a new style of fiction and he described *The Magic of Wealth* as a 'Vehicle of Opinions'. The particular aspect of the book that may have caught Jane Austen's attention is in the story of its villain, Mr Flim-Flam, a tradesman grown rich and turned banker, who exploits the current fashion for seaside resorts and changes the fishing village of Thistleton into Flimflampton. This part of the story is probably modelled on actual events: the change, in the 1790s, of the fishing village of Bognor, by a rich London hatter, Edward Hotham, who named the new resort Hothampton. The speculation was a notable disaster and

Hothampton became Bognor once again. Flim-Flam is a speculator and projector fired by a 'rage for building' which destroys old England, represented in the Manor House, and puts up in its place a rash of 'gee-gaw' villas. His main opponent is Mr Oldways, whose 'ruling passion' is 'To sustain unsullied the reputation of a gentleman of family and fortune ... Born and bred the true old English gentleman, he possessed no particle of the trafficking spirit of the times'.

Surr states these positions very baldly; the hero and the villain are mouthpieces; and altogether the novel is an underfictionalised piece of propaganda, specifically against the recent introduction of bank-notes, scathingly called paper money. Tory political economists believed that this easy way of creating wealth (the 'Magic' of the title) was at the root of the country's social problems. It placed power in the hands of the financiers at the expense of the landed gentry, the traditional guardians of the country's stability and its social health. Surr was a banker himself and had his own axes to grind. But his general argument faithfully reflects a widespread anxiety at this change. It is one of the central points in Coleridge's *A Lay Sermon* (Mar 1817), where he laments that post-war conditions made it impossible 'for the gentry of the land, for the possessors of fixed property to retain the rank of their ancestors, or their own former establishments, without joining in the general competition under the influence of the same trading spirit'. A gentleman, he declares, 'ought not to regard his estate as a merchant his cargo, or a shopkeeper his stock'. For Coleridge, and many other commentators, the selling up of family estates represented the destruction of cherished values in English society; it marked the triumph of modern profit over the tradition of stewardship which had preserved estates intact from generation to generation.

In the eyes of traditionalists and reactionaries, seaside resorts were an elegant but depressing symbol of the new cash nexus – a relationship devoid of humanity. Unlike the humble fishing villages they replaced, the resorts had no dependance on the life of the land or the sea. Their raison d'être was in the frenzy and triviality of fashion, what Cobbett diagnosed as the 'morbid restlessness' of the age, later materialised in the mushroom growth of such towns as Brighton:

a place of no trade; of no commerce at all; it has no harbour, it is no place of deposit or transit for corn or for goods or cattle: ...

the valleys and sides of hills, now covered with elegant houses,
were formerly cornfields, and downs for the pasture of sheep. Very
pretty is the town and its virandas and carriages, and harnessed
goats; very pretty to *behold*; but dismal to think of ...

(*Rural Rides*, Brighton, 28 July 1832)

These arguments are lightly and allusively contained in *Sanditon*.
Mr Parker's eloquence is borrowed from the rhetorical flights of the
coastal guide-books and the sales-talk of the seaside medical tribe;
Mr Heywood is a country Cobbett, seeing another 'dismal' Brighton
in prospect; and the theories of the political economists are fed into
their debate about the effect of the new resorts on prices and on the
state of the poor. With Lady Denham, Mr Parker is led into a more
detailed exposition of the laws of supply and demand and the level
of prices and rents, in order to convince her that the arrival of a
free-spending 'West-Indy' family will not strike Sanditon with
inflation and that as a property-owner, she stands to benefit from
the prosperity of the tradesmen. Mr Parker's advocacy is fluent and
half-baked. Like Arthur Parker's speculations of the Physics of
Perspiration, his flourish of theory comes from one of the contemporary digests of knowledge which equipped ladies and gentlemen
with conversational lines with which to edify and impress their
friends. The display of scientific knowledge and social theory was
the latest accomplishment of an improved society, a sign of its
advance.

The 'Charitable hearts' and 'Benevolence' of the Parker sisters
are also involved in the improvement joke, for the rise of philanthropy, of organised charity, was another attribute of Regency
enlightenment. Formerly, charity had existed in the support of one's
friends and neighbours and in the patronage of the local squire, a
relationship that lingers on in old-world Highbury. But with the
growth of towns, this informal system began to disappear and people
with a social conscience, particularly the Methodists and Evangeli-
cals, began to fill the gap. Very soon, charity work became fashionable. As the novelist Mrs Barbauld remarked in 1813, it was inspired
'not so much from a sense of duty as being the real taste of the
times'. There was social kudos in belonging to a charitable com-
mittee; and charitable activities were also a convenient method
of easing the middle-class conscience about its prosperous and
pleasure-seeking way of life in an age of poverty and starvation.
This bitter contrast was even more sharply defined after 1814, with

the rising price of bread, and destitution swollen by returning soldiers for whom there was no work. In *The Magic of Wealth* Surr draws an ugly picture of contemporary conscience-salving at Flim-flampton, where subscription dinners and entertainments are organised to raise funds: 'a most grotesque and absurd conjunction of mirth and pity – of gaiety and compassion. Pleasure may be the real motive; but Philanthropy must be the pass-word, even to our amusements'. There is no trace of anger in Jane Austen's account of Diana Parker. Nevertheless, the portrait is ruthlessly exact. This is the type of society woman for whom charity is not a matter of the human heart but an occupation, a business in life, as compulsive and driving as the manic enthusiasm of her brother, and far less endearing. She practises charity at long distance; her causes, scattered around the land, are displayed like a collection of trophies. This is fashionable philanthropy, expressed in terms of getting Lady Denham to head the list of subscribers. Jane Austen saw no need to underline the point of this satire and she had already provided her readers with a model of true charity in *Persuasion*, in the help that the sickly Mrs Smith struggles to give 'one or two very poor families' in the neighbourhood of Westgate Buildings, and that small detail is within the entire episode of Anne Elliot's visiting, a charity of sympathy which is private, undisplayed and face-to-face; which is, in these respects, *un*fashionable and, as far as her father is concerned, disgracefully *infra dig*.

In its detailed social and literary reference, *Sanditon* is the most packed and concentrated of all Jane Austen's novels. Allusion is one of its methods and also one of its jokes. Undoubtedly, Jane Austen delighted in the sheer virtuosity of her performance in mimicking so many styles of writing and calling up such a variety of literary and social types. The joke even runs to self-parody. One of the artistic feats of *Mansfield Park* is the way in which the visit to Sotherton and the rehearsals for *Lovers' Vows* are used to foreshadow the pattern of events and relationships that arise later in the novel. In the comedy of errors at the opening of *Sanditon*, Jane Austen plays with this same device. Mr Parker's coach founders up an impassable lane; his ankle unexpectedly fails under him; his wild goose chase for the Willingden surgeon, pursued with such obstinacy and optimism, ends in a confusion of muddle and cross-purposes. In modern critical terminology, this episode would be described as a sequence of anticipatory symbolic action, announcing Sanditon's future:

A very few years ago, & it had been a quiet Village of no preten-
sions; but some natural advantages in its position & some accidental circumstances having suggested to himself, & the other
principal Land Holder, the probability of it's becoming a profitable
Speculation, they had engaged in it, & planned & built, & praised
& puffed, & raised it to a something of young Renown ... (p. 371)

Sanditon is a Regency South Sea Bubble and Jane Austen foretells
its fate in the burlesque comedy of the opening pages, a joke which
is also turned against her own sophistication of literary technique.

Alongside this allusive mode of satire, Jane Austen also conducts
an easy-going descriptive level of local comedy in showing how the
'Spirit of the day', the tide of improvement, is sweeping the village
– the fishermen's cottages now 'smartened up', the 'old Farm House'
now adorned by 'two Females in elegant white ... with their books
& camp stools', the baker's shop now regaled by 'the sound of a
Harp' from above, and in the shoemaker's window 'Civilization'
arrived in the shape of 'Blue Shoes, & nankin Boots!' (p. 383).
Improvement has carried the Parkers away from the snug comfort
of their old house, the home of Mr Parker's 'Forefathers', and
brought them up the hill, to 'modern Sanditon', to their new home,
Trafalgar House, 'a light elegant Building, standing in a small Lawn
with a very young plantation round it' (p. 384). Here, Mr Parker
boasts, he can enjoy 'all the Grandeur of the Storm, with less real
danger' (p. 381) – a modern, romantic appreciation of the sea,
touched with old-world prudence. The scales are weighed against
Trafalgar House. For all its lightness and elegance, it stands in
opposition to Mr Parker's old home, the home of his forefathers,
another Donwell Abbey, 'well fenced & planted, & rich in the
Garden, Orchard & Meadows which are the best embellishments of
such a dwelling' (p. 379), a snug and comfortable house, which
Mrs Parker regrets leaving. Nonetheless, Trafalgar House commands
a view. When Charlotte Heywood looks out of her window for the
first time, over Sanditon and out to the sea, her impression is real
and vivid – not Mr Parker's stormy grandeur, not those '*undescrib-
able* Emotions' which 'the Sea & the Sea shore' should 'excite in the
Mind of Sensibility' (p. 396), according to Sir Edward Denham, but
a scene whose vitality and charm belong to this present moment in
Sanditon's development: 'the miscellaneous foreground of unfinished
Buildings, waving Linen, & tops of Houses, to the Sea, dancing &
sparkling in Sunshine & Freshness' (p. 384). This is the clear and

immediate vision of a heroine whose mind is uncontaminated by the new theories of romanticism or by the old theories of sentiment and the picturesque. Charlotte Heywood looks at Sanditon with the uneducated eye of youth, ready to be interested and amused, a point of view that carries the writer's own responsiveness to the phenomena of improvement.

But the delightful and decorative 'spirit of the day' that breathes over Sanditon has another face in the 'spirit of restless activity' that Charlotte Heywood diagnoses as the fever of the Parker sisters. Sanditon has a local and transitory beauty, the charm of the moment. But there is frenzy to its creation. Charlotte tries to puzzle out the dynamics of the Parker family and concludes that all their frenetic exertions – Mr Parker's as a 'Projector', the sisters in their 'extraordinary' revolution of 'Disorders & Recoveries', and in their 'Zeal for being useful' – come from an excess of energy and an absence of anything to do (p. 412). Here, Jane Austen puts her finger on the occupational disease of the gentry: prosperous and leisured, they had nothing to do. Hence the pursuit of pleasure and the rise of Sanditon. The Parkers are the agents of change, intoxicated by their own wild and wayward energies. To adopt a phrase from Shelley, 'the electric life' that runs through them is 'less their own spirit than the spirit of their age'. Cobbett's 'morbid restlessness' is Jane Austen's 'spirit of restless activity' whose erratic momentum is felt in these characters and throughout the fragment in the story's tempo, in its violence of movement and in its extremities of style.

Some recent historical critics place Jane Austen as an essentially eighteenth-century writer, and there has been a further attempt at categorisation, labelling her as a traditionalist with the values and attitudes of a Tory-Augustan. Certainly, there is a mid-eighteenth-century foundation to her moral vision and to the style of its expression. Johnson and Cowper are never far away and Cowper's views on seaside resorts and the strengths and virtues of old-world rustic simplicity are alluded to in *Sanditon*.[10] An amusing strain of eighteenth-century decorum informs Charlotte Heywood's primness, which is both an affirmation and a joke. This decorum also extends into the language and metaphors of *Sanditon*, with the effect of a delicate and ladylike constraint, a stylistic holding-back, played off against energies of character and expression which are wilder and freer. Jane Austen's commitment is not partisan: she has no causes to argue in the manner of Cobbett or Surr, nor any breath of Coleridge's grave indignation and urgency. Her commitment is artistic: to the hilarious comedy of eccentricity, extravagance and collision, and to the subtler tensions of uncertainty and change. Her personal roots and sympathies lie with Mr Heywood; his 'very quiet, settled, careful course of Life' in the country, 'rendered pleasant by Habit' (p. 374), is the very situation in which she was able to work best, as we know from the way in which her creative drive returned as soon as she settled at Chawton Cottage in 1809.[11] But part of Jane Austen's continuing triumph as a writer was her openness to fresh experience and her readiness to explore new means for its expression.

In the Harcourt Brace students' edition of *Pride and Prejudice*, Bradford Booth includes as a contextualising piece one of Washington Irving's essays on Regency life. It provides an extremely interesting account of the inter-linkings in the structure of English society and the position, within this, of country houses like Pemberley, seen through the eyes of a visitor from the new world, fascinated, as later in the century Henry James was to be, by the cultural antiquity of the old. 'The great charm' Irving discovered in the English landscape, something more than its 'captivating loveliness', was what he defines as 'the moral feeling that seems to pervade it. It is associated in the mind with ideas of order, of quiet, of sober well-established principles, of hoary usage and reverend custom'; and he goes on to describe an ancient church, a village and an old manor-house: 'all these common features of English landscape evince a calm and settled security, and hereditary transmission of home-bred virtues and local attachments, that speak deeply and touchingly for the moral character of the nation.'[12] Less sweepingly, less grandiosely, Jane Austen's unimproved houses and grounds belong to Irving's theme. But her inclination towards the traditional order of country neighbourhoods unimproved is never transposed into such a static, sentimental idyllicism as Irving indulges in. Indeed, Jane Austen is nostalgic about the past. But it is a nostalgia that she admits to, just as she admits to the attraction of improvement, the very thing that threatens the past, just as she admits to her own insecurity in the pull of these forces. In *The Statesman's Manual* (1816) Coleridge speaks of 'that restless craving for the wonders of the day'. This is a craving to which Jane Austen's imagination was not immune, and *Sanditon* is a confession to the beguiling power of the new 'wonders' of the Regency-Romantic age and a testimony to the continuing freshness and inventiveness of her response.

AFTERNOTE

This essay is a literary critic's attempt at historical interpretation. Predictably, at the Alberta Conference, where it was first delivered, its thesis was questioned. In particular, David Spring of Johns Hopkins University wondered whether the period of Jane Austen's lifetime really was such a watershed in English history, between the so-called 'old' society and the 'new', as I claim here. My only answer to this can be to refer to the contemporary commentators and historians who supposed that such a change was taking place, and to Jane Austen herself (see, for example, her account of this change as it is seen in the different generations of the Musgrove family, quoted here p. 7). But Professor Spring's concern is to be welcomed, as is that of any historian, since to my knowledge only Harold Perkin, Professor of Social History at the University of Lancaster, has provided any account of this question (in *The Origins of Modern English Society 1780–1880*, London, 1969). I should stress, however, that his analysis is purely historical and extra-literary and that the account I offer here was informed but not guided by his book. My starting point was in Jane Austen and the excursion into history was directed by issues that seemed to be raised in the text. It is very possible, as Professor Spring suggests, that I have been guilty of misunderstanding or misemphasis; and in that case, my attempt will at least have drawn attention to some of the pitfalls that literary interpretation can encounter on historical terrain. So this note can be taken as an appeal for the historians to offer us a helping hand. More and more critics are venturing into this (to them) strange territory and Jane Austen studies seem set on a historical course for some years to come.

NOTES

1 I belong to the former group and my argument for regarding the manuscript as a developed work is set out in Chapter 7 of *Jane Austen's Literary Manuscripts* (London, 1964).

2 *The Nation and the Athenaeum*, 21 Mar 1925, p. 860; reprinted in *Abinger Harvest* (London, 1936).

3 *Jane Austen: Irony as Defense and Discovery* (Princeton, N.J., 1952) pp. 257–8.

4 Alistair Duckworth has explored the house-and-grounds aspect extensively in *The Improvement of the Estate: A Study of Jane Austen's Novels* (Baltimore and London, 1971). With the availability of a facsimile edition of *Sanditon*

(ed. B. C. Southam, London, 1975) readers will be able to come to their own conclusions on this question.

5 Entry for 20 Aug 1791.

6 Count von Rumford (Sir Benjamin Thompson), *Essays, Political, Economical, and Philosophical* (London, 1796) I, p. 197.

7 *The Complete Works of Count Rumford* (Boston, 1870–5) II, p. 485.

8 Ibid., IV, p. 452.

9 In fact, green tea is a narcotic and does affect the nervous system; and Jane Austen's joke is not so very far-fetched: in the *Times Literary Supplement* (19 Sep 1975, p. 1063), Miss Elizabeth Suddaby cites an instance of green tea being studied scientifically during Jane Austen's lifetime and of its causing paralysis in an arm.

10 Mary Lascelles has pointed out that the discussion between Mr and Mrs Parker about the best situation for a house seems to take up points from *The Task* (1784), where Cowper makes fun of improvers. *Jane Austen and her Art* (London, 1939) p. 46.

11 In the eight years previously, Jane Austen had lived an unsettled and unproductive existence in a succession of temporary homes. As soon as she came to Chawton Cottage, where she remained until 1817, she took up the manuscripts of *Sense and Sensibility* and *Pride and Prejudice* to get them ready for publication.

12 First published in *The Sketchbook*, 1819–20. Reprinted in Bradford Booth's edition of *Pride and Prejudice* (New York, 1963) p. 179.

2 The Business of Marrying and Mothering

LLOYD W. BROWN

My title has a double source in Jane Austen's writings. It derives, in part, from the description of Mrs Bennet as a woman whose business in life 'was to get her daughters married' (*P&P*, p. 5), and from a letter to Fanny Knight in which the novelist advises her niece on the advantages of marriage in later rather than earlier womanhood: 'by not beginning the business of Mothering quite so early in life', she writes consolingly, 'you will be young in Constitution, spirits, figure & countenance, while Mrs Wm Hammond is growing old by confinements & nursing' (*Letters*, p. 483). My objective is to clarify the precise implications of marriage and motherhood in both her correspondence and her fiction, especially in so far as those views contribute to an understanding of Austen's perception of women and society as a whole. Clearly our times have heightened the significance of such views, although they have always attracted critical attention in the study of the novels. Indeed in a certain historical perspective few of our current approaches to Austen's women are essentially new, notwithstanding the suspicion that many of them have been motivated in one way or the other by an academic 'fall-out' of sorts from the contemporary women's movements. Hence as early as 1938 Mona Wilson offers as frank a feminist reading of the novels as we are likely to obtain in our own time, and after twenty years Mark Schorer's overview of marriage in *Pride and Prejudice* is still unsurpassed in its emphasis on Austen's decidedly unromantic and realistic perception of marriage as a 'brutal economic fact in an essentially materialistic society.' Significantly enough Schorer's study and his own language tend to reinforce Austen's own description of marriage and motherhood as forms of business: *Pride and Prejudice* is 'a novel about marriage as a market, and about the female as marketable.'[1]

Nonetheless it is indisputable that this aspect of Austen's fiction has been attracting increasing attention along a fairly wide front that ranges from the usual character analysis of the textual critic to post-Freudian speculations about her attitudes to marriage and child-bearing.[2] Perhaps few subjects have been discussed in these current studies with more frequency and intensity than the significance of marriage in the lives of Austen's women. But on the whole one senses that the novelist's perception of marriage, and motherhood, are rather more complex than either of the alternative views that are usually offered: that is, marriage is either a socio-economic pact to which Austen is wholly unsympathetic, or it is the climax and celebration of moral and emotional maturity. Despite ignoring some of Austen's reservations about marriage, especially in her correspondence, C. A. Linder hints at the complexity by noting that Austen appears to view marriage simultaneously as the woman's socio-economic convenience and, particularly in the case of the Crofts, as an equally shared experience based on an affinity of interests rather than on the subordination of the woman as mere housekeeper.[3] More specifically, however, what I am concerned with here is an apparent paradox in the handling of marriage and motherhood in Austen's work. On the one hand, matrimony is not only the inevitable *sine qua non* of each dénouement, but it is also the desirable goal of each heroine. Even Emma in her misogamist phase is quite confident about the desirability of marriage – for everybody else of course. But on the other hand, there is a virtual absence of any perception of marriage *per se* as a fulfilling experience, apart from the symbolic role of celebrating the maturation of the protagonist's perception and relationship. And, on the surface at any rate, it is remarkable that so many marriages are disaster areas in works that lead their main protagonists to the inevitable felicity of *connubial* happy endings. In the case of motherhood, 'natural' (as distinct from substitute) mothers are nearly all inept or worse as parents. Interestingly enough the rarely effective mother figures of the novels function in this regard with respect to young women who are not their own offspring. Mrs Gardiner's role vis-à-vis Elizabeth Bennet is the most typical of these relationships. And in *Sense and Sensibility* we eventually discover a genuinely attractive warmth and level-headedness beneath Mrs Jennings' cheerful vulgarity, but these qualities seem to be more effective in her relationships with Marianne and Elinor than with her own daughter. Conversely, 'adoptive' or substitute mothers of this kind tend to be more ineffective, even undesirable, in direct proportion to the degree to which they replace natural mothers. Lady Bertram is as hopeless a mother for Fanny Price as she is for her own offspring. Mrs Weston, who is the only 'mother' that Emma has known for most of her life, clearly has to share some of the blame for Emma's failings. And by a similar token Lady Russell is considerably less than reliable when she substitutes for Anne Elliott's late mother. This parental failure (which extends to fathers) does raise questions about Austen's attitude towards motherhood as such, notwithstanding the settled comfort of Marianne Dashwood as mother or Emma's presumed dedication to the task of providing Donwell Abbey with an heir.

Austen's letters offer some important insights into this apparent paradox because they clearly present personal views which, taken together, represent a complex of attitudes that are highly pertinent, in the long run, to the significance of marriage and motherhood in the novels. On the whole the comments on marriage and motherhood are substantial and pointed enough, especially in the letters to Fanny Knight, who seems not only to have been a favourite niece, but also a very special correspondent – largely, one suspects, because the younger woman impressed her aunt as an intelligent, self-assured, and enormously warm-hearted person. First, Austen offers Fanny the time-honoured caveats against the loveless marriage. 'Anything is to be preferred or endured rather than marrying without Affection,' she warns in one letter (*Letters*, p. 410). And in another she adds, 'Nothing can be compared to the misery of being bound *without* Love, bound to one, & preferring another. *That* is a Punishment which you do *not* deserve' (p. 418). The letters to Cassandra are more flippantly phrased, but their emphasis is really the same as those to Fanny. 'Lady Sondes' match surprises, but does not offend me,' she confides; 'had her first marriage been of affection, or had there been a grown-up single daughter, I should not have forgiven her; but I consider everybody as having a right to marry *once* in their lives for love, if they can, and provided she will now leave off having bad headaches and being pathetic, I can allow her, I can *wish* her, to be happy' (p. 240).

Secondly, notwithstanding that veiled barb at Lady Sondes' earlier marriage of convenience, Austen is very aware of the importance of such marriages to single women in her society, particularly women whose economic circumstances leave them with marriage as the only recourse for survival in a society in which recourses for the single woman's survival are very few indeed. When she does mention one popular alternative to the loveless marriage of survival – employment as a governess – her pitying tone recalls Mrs Elton on Jane

Fairfax's prospects as a governess. Miss Allen, the governess of Anna Austen's daughters, wins her sympathy: 'poor creature! I pity her, tho' they *are* my neices' (p. 278). In the light of all this it is not surprising that when she considers the single woman's lack of economic independence or choices, Austen's preference for the love-match is intertwined with an awareness of the very understandable motives behind a marriage of convenience, at least from the view-point of a relatively poor woman like Molly Milles: 'I ... must feel for Miss Milles, though she *is* Molly, if a material loss of Income is to attend her other loss. – Single women have a dreadful propensity for being poor – which is one very strong argument in favour of Matrimony' (p. 483). Clearly none of this amounts to a rejection of the advice which she offers Fanny during this same period against the loveless marriage. But the tone of these letters on the socio-economic disadvantages of being poor, single, and female strongly suggests that her perception of marriage in the woman's situation as a whole is more complex than a simple, straightforward distinction between love-matches and marriages of convenience. There is a marked ambivalence here towards the significance of marriage in the woman's emotional life, her socio-economic environment, and in her total sense of individuality.

On a third level, however, this kind of ambivalence gives way to an outright scepticism about individuals and marriages as they usually are. Quite simply, defective persons make defective marriages. There are enough unsatisfactory marriages to support such a maxim, and in the correspondence we are left with the impression that prevailing social manners have engendered a breed of women (and men) whose inadequacies compound the inherent difficulties of marriage. In this vein, her jibe at a new bride's '*parade* of happiness' (p. 411) is comparable with the ridicule of Mrs Elton's 'apparatus of happiness' at the Donwell Abbey picnic (*E*, p. 358). For, quite apart from those moral and intellectual shortcomings which make for unsatisfactory marriages, there are certain habits which Austen seems to attribute specifically to women. That 'parade of happiness' which she deplores in a letter to Fanny Knight is a habit that she has often encountered in the letters of 'young married Women'. Indeed several of Austen's letters return repeatedly to those female eccentricities which irritated or amused her. For example, she is decidedly entertained by the discovery that young Mr Wildman, a friend of Fanny Knight, is determined to foster idealistic images of women: 'I particularly respect him for wishing to think well of all young Ladies; it shews an amiable & a delicate Mind. – And he deserves better treatment than to be obliged to read any more of my Works' (*Letters*, p. 487). She herself is unsparing of chattering beauties, gossipy back-biters, and determined hypochondriacs. In the last group Lady Sondes of the bad headaches is joined by, among others, Mrs Edward Bridges, 'a poor Honey – the sort of woman who gives me the idea of being determined never to be well – & who likes her spasms & nervousness & the consequence they give her, better than anything else' (p. 339). The generic implications of the phrase, 'sort of woman', are as significant as the parallel with Mrs Bennet's famous nerves. The possibilities for generally humane and rewarding relationships in marriage are blunted by the individual's failings (including female insecurities) as well as by the mercenary realities that arise from the woman's traditional dependency.

Austen's letters go beyond all of this to raise another issue. Quite apart from the individual and social shortcomings which affect marital relationships adversely, marriage is itself an intrinsically suspect institution. It dampens the personality, especially the female personality. And this seems to be true, not merely of the flaccid characters of chattering beauties, but even of estimable and sturdy personalities like Fanny Knight. Consequently the letter which praises Fanny for her intelligence, imagination, and warm-heartedness also regrets the likelihood that she will eventually be married: 'Oh! what a loss it will be when you are married. You are too agreable in your single state, too agreable as a Neice. I shall hate you when your delicious play of Mind is all settled down into conjugal & maternal affections' (pp. 478–9). Clearly, Austen is suggesting that marriage as an institution encourages a sense of roles, and that this role-consciousness subordinates even the complex personality of a Fanny Knight to the predetermined patterns of conjugal and maternal roles. To sum up, marriage as love-match involves the celebration of individual maturity and represents a shared equality, but at the same time the very nature of marriage imbues the relationship with a sense of role-playing that inevitably has a subordinating effect on the woman's personality.

The inclusion of motherhood in the context of her letter to Fanny Knight is highly pertinent here because it reinforces the claims of that letter to Fanny in which Austen attributes the early loss of youth, spirits, and health to the 'business of mothering'. Childbearing, or to be more specific, the inevitable chain of successive confinements, invariably repels Austen. 'Poor Woman!' she exclaims of Mrs Tilson. 'How can she be honestly breeding again?' (p. 210). When she refers to Anna Austen's frequent pregnancies there is a note of pity, the feeling that woman as perpetual breeder is a trapped animal: 'Anna has not a chance of escape. . . . Poor Animal, she will be worn out before she is thirty. – I am very sorry for her. – Mrs Clement too is in that way again. I am quite tired of so many Children. – Mrs Benn has a thirteenth' (p. 488). And on another occasion she sarcastically suggests a birth-control device for the prolific Mr and Mrs Deedes – 'the simple regimen of separate rooms' (p. 480). It is true enough that the high rate of fatal confinements in her time may have influenced Austen's concern with the disadvantages of child-bearing. But clearly she is more concerned in letters like this with the reduced lives of those who survive one confinement to move on inexorably to another, then another. It is tempting enough to fall back on that old adage about the childless woman's 'envy of the maternal role', but read in conjunction with her remarks about the suppressive nature of pre-determined roles in the woman's experience, Austen seems to be more preoccupied here with the suspicion that motherhood as she knew it in her society seemed incompatible with the physical and intellectual vigour of the unmarried and childless woman. Austen's obvious delight in her role as aunt (she mentions this more than once to Fanny) implies that she is not averse to a maternal relationship of sorts, the aunt-as-mother relationship which links Elizabeth Bennet and Mrs Gardiner. But on balance the maternal role is a mixed blessing or a necessary evil at best. Like marriage, it remains a business, complete with its physical cost to the woman and with role responsibilities that exact their toll on her individuality.

On the whole what we find in these letters amounts to the de-romanticising, or demystification, of marriage and motherhood without the unequivocal rejection of either. From the idealist's viewpoint marriage is the ritualistic symbol of those emotional and intellectual values that are joined in the mutual respect of the love-match. On a realistic level society may counterbalance, even thwart, the ideal possibilities of the love-match by way of those socio-economic disadvantages which make the marriage of convenience a match of necessity. In a similar vein, if marriage represents the promising union of vibrant individualists like Fanny Knight, it also becomes a damper on the woman's individualism. Altogether there is an ambivalence here which represents a tension between Austen's idealism and her hard-headed realism, and which is evident in the treatment of marriage and motherhood in the novels. The function of marriage as a symbolic celebration has been receiving increasing attention in the novels: the marriage of an Austen heroine signalises the achievement of a self-sufficient and mature individualism on both sides, and as such it underscores the full equality on which the relationship is now based, and which critics are now seeing as Austen's essential feminism.[4] But side by side with the realization of the feminist ideal in the marriages of her heroines we find a frank recognition of those socio-economic facts of life upon which Austen comments in her letters. This kind of recognition has immediate implications for a work like *Sense and Sensibility*. The repulsiveness of Lucy Steele's cold-blooded quest for a profitable match, *any* profitable match, is obvious enough. So is her sister's vulgar eagerness. But the precarious situation of the single woman with limited means encourages our simultaneous understanding of their motives. Conversely, Elinor Dashwood's marriage, while safely distanced from the narrowly mercenary prudence of her brother's world, still respects the socially determined requirement of prudent matches for poor women. And, to extend this argument to the thematic structure of *Sense and Sensibility* as a whole, Elinor's marriage to Edward Ferrars unites the private emotional sensibilities of the love-match with the good sense that deals realistically with the externally imposed rules of the social order.

Moreover Miss Bates' situation commands our sympathies precisely because she is a living example of the single woman's 'dreadful propensity for being poor'. And nothwithstanding Elizabeth Bennet's justified indignation at Charlotte Lucas' frank opportunism, the socio-economic realities which are so clear-cut in *Pride and Prejudice* require from us a more complex reaction to Charlotte's acceptance of Mr Collins' proposal of marriage. This is the kind of reaction that includes but goes beyond Elizabeth's straightforward moral indignation; for in light of those socio-economic realities Charlotte's sense of choice has been severely limited from the start. Her marriage is not simply an intellectual and moral lapse. It is also a pathetic reflection of her situation and the situation of young women like herself. She invites both our censure and our sympathy. Marriage ought to be a full, complex, human relationship, but for women like Charlotte it is also a business of sorts. On this basis, the narrative ironies of *Pride and Prejudice* may be partially traced to the business of Mrs Bennet's life – the business of marrying her daughters. Her neuroses as wife and mother are ludicrous enough. But the fact remains that to a considerable degree the events of the plot do satisfy her ambition – in spite of her own best efforts of course. And in the light of Austen's personal concern about the single woman's limited choices, we may very well discover a complex reaction on our part to Mrs Bennet's obsession with the entailment of the Longbourn estate. To this end the novel holds up marriage both as an ideally fulfilling goal and as the single woman's socially determined business. This remains so even in the supposedly mellower atmosphere of *Persuasion* where the 'bad morality' of the imprudent love-match is defended by the author (p. 248). But in the long run this kind of moral absoluteness is defensible and attractive only as an ideal hypothesis in the narrative as a whole. After all, despite Anne Elliot's regret about *her* youthful prudence, and despite the narrator's salute to impoverished young lovers, the fact remains that Anne's marriage enjoys the reassuring basis of Captain Wentworth's independent fortune, together with the couple's good qualities of mind and spirit: 'their maturity of mind, consciousness of right, and one independent fortune between them' (p. 248).

On a more satiric level the ideally fulfilling marriages of the heroines are outnumbered by marriages which are failures. Such failures are not necessarily defined by unhappiness or non-communication as such, though this is obviously so in several cases. The parting shot at Willoughby and his marriage is more than a final jibe at the sentimental reader: 'that he was for ever inconsolable, that he fled from society, or contracted an habitual gloom of temper, or died of a broken heart, must not be depended on – for he did neither.' It is also a pointed emphasis on the very real, as opposed to sentimentally conceived, shortcomings which make his marriage a continuing punishment of sorts for past indiscretion and insensitivity. For the description of his 'domestic felicity' with the shrewish Miss Morton is couched in a series of suggestive understatements that are supplemented by the even more revealing references to the real sources of his felicity – horses, dogs and sports rather than the marriage itself: 'He lived to exert, and frequently to enjoy himself. His wife was not always out of humour, nor his home always uncomfortable; and in his breed of horses and dogs, and in sporting of every kind, he found no inconsiderable degree of domestic felicity' (*S&S*, p. 379). In *Pride and Prejudice* the scathing dismissal of the Wickhams offers a striking contrast with the ideal implications of Elizabeth's marriage: 'His affection for her soon sunk into indifference; her's lasted a little longer; and in spite of her youth and her manners, she retained all the claims to reputation which her marriage had given her' (p. 387). In view of the unsavoury personalities of both Lydia and Wickham this emphasis on their marital failure could easily be limited to the moral implications of their characters were it not for the fact that theirs is simply one more marital failure in the novel. In fact all the marriages that are dealt with in any significant detail (and this would exclude the Gardiners) are inadequate. Charlotte Lucas is no less aware than is the reader of the severe limitations of her marriage. And in the Bennets' marriage Austen offers a chilling analysis of what amounts to a malaise, one which not only ensures the failure of the Bennets' marriage but seems certain of repetition in the next generation of couples, the Collinses and Wickhams, for example:

> Had Elizabeth's opinion been all drawn from her own family, she could not have formed a very pleasing picture of conjugal felicity or domestic comfort. Her father captivated by youth and beauty, and that appearance of good humour, which youth and beauty generally give, had married a woman whose weak understanding and illiberal mind, had very early in their marriage put an end to all real affection for her. Respect, esteem, and confidence, had vanished for ever; and all his views of domestic happiness were overthrown. ... He was fond of the country and of books; and from these tastes had arisen his principal enjoyments. To his wife he was very little otherwise indebted, than as her ignorance and folly had contributed to his amusement. This is not the sort of happiness which a man would in general wish to owe to his wife; but where other powers of entertainment are wanting, the true philosopher will derive benefit from such as are given. (p. 236)

Even those marriages in which the couples seem reasonably satisfied and compatible are also disturbing because they too imply a questionable continuity. Taken together compatible but deficient couples represent the continuation of their inadequacies within an institutional context (marriage) in much the same way that the conflicts and non-communication of the Bennets represent a pervasive and continuous malaise in human values and relationships. The perfect compatibility of the John Dashwoods, for example, rests in the cold-blooded materialism and in the narrow selfishness which they share equally. But more to the point, that compatibility and the marital continuity which it assures throughout the novel underscore the vigour and persistence of the Dashwoods' value system in their society. Elinor's and Marianne's marriages represent ideal exceptions. The Dashwoods' union is demonstrably a symbolic extension of the prevailing rule: it is part of a total pattern over which their formidable ally Mrs Ferrars presides to the end. Like the Dashwoods themselves the Dashwood marriage is static and mechanical, and that mechanicality reflects the unyielding hardness of the narrow 'sense' which dominates their world and which is also symbolised by the unions of Robert Ferrars and Lucy Steele, Willoughby and Miss Morton, Sir John and Lady Middleton, and Mr and Mrs Palmer. In identifying these defective unions with prevailing social norms Austen is not simply establishing marriage as a symbol of a social malaise, she is also demonstrating that defective marriages of all kinds (like those of the Bennets or the Dashwoods) continue because their causes are rooted in the continuing defects of their social institutions and environment. By a similar token the Elton marriage in *Emma* is doubly disturbing because Mr Elton's role as vicar (like that of Mr Collins in *Pride and Prejudice*) emphasises that the individual defects may be embodied and perpetuated, however undesignedly, by established institutions – marriage *and* the church in this case – through individuals whose moral and intellectual limitations have defined the actual, as opposed to the ideal, functions of these institutions.

The implication here is that the ideal possibilities that are inherent in the growth and marriage of the Austen heroine must be viewed in isolation from those shortcomings which influence individual and society, and which are confirmed as *continuing* norms (limited individualism, moral meanness, intellectual shallowness, emotional narrowness, and so forth). In fact the very nature of the heroine's development and the related significance of her marriage tend to present her and her male counterpart as exceptional persons, or at the very least as individuals who have achieved a level of awareness that makes them unusual, even unique, in their society. This partly explains the isolation which seems to mark the Austen heroine. Even Catherine Morland's personality is pertinent here. The parodic contrasts (with the typical Gothic heroine) through which she is initially introduced have the effect of comically isolating her childhood and early upbringing from the usual heroine's role of the fine lady. And, more pointedly, her eventual maturation is accompanied by a sense of separateness from the limited Isabella Thorpes of her world. In *Sense and Sensibility* Elinor's feelings tend to be overlooked equally by Austen's readers and by Elinor's family precisely because she really has no one in her circle who fully equals her eventual synthesis of feeling and reason; and because of this she feels an isolation which does not allow her a free self-expression. Interestingly, Anne Elliot, the most mature and sensible of Austen's heroines, is also her most isolated. And even Elizabeth Bennet, although she enjoys close ties with her father, older sister, and her aunt, is presented explicitly as an exceptional person in her world. As she playfully reminds Darcy towards the close of the novel, he was attracted to her precisely because she was so unusual in comparison with the more conventional women who fawned on him for his attention in the past (*P&P*, p. 380). And it is in this work that Austen is most explicit in her preference for the unusual woman, the woman with rare capacities for growth and individual self-sufficiency, rather than the average woman whose personality is shaped by prevailing notions of woman as the subordinate sex. Elizabeth therefore fits the self-sufficient role, probably because, in Mrs Bennet's plaintive words, she has been allowed to 'run ... wild' at home (p. 42). Mrs Bennet's language recalls Mary Wollstonecraft's description of the kind of self-education through which a few young women achieved a level of individuality in lieu of the standard education for young 'ladies'.[5]

Austen's apparent preoccupation with unusually individualistic women has a significant bearing on her perception of marriage and motherhood in the woman's experience and in society as a whole. By limiting individual maturity to women who are demonstrably unusual in their circle Austen implies a somewhat sceptical view of the possibilities of change in society at large. On the surface at any rate it would appear that this scepticism has been softened or replaced in *Persuasion*, where Anne's marriage is not exceptional within the novel as such, but is actually complemented by the marriages of the Harvilles and the Crofts. But naval marriages like these bear a suggestively outside or alien image because their naval background somehow establishes a symbolically physical distance from prevailing social norms for marriage. And in a more literal sense, sailors and their women *are* outsiders: their occupation and environment represent a spatial openness which seems to encourage a more liberated sense of self and others than one encounters in the fixed, narrower conventions of the rest of society. Consequently, despite Louisa Musgrove's penchant for the suspect hyperbole, her encomium on the navy (apropos of the happy Harville marriage) smacks a great deal of Austen's known prejudices in favour of the navy: 'Louisa ... was convinced of sailors having more worth and warmth than any other set of men in England; that they only knew how to live, and they only deserved to be respected and loved' (p. 99). Mrs Croft's marriage and temper (she is impatient with men who treat women as fine ladies rather than rational creatures) confirm the mature individuality and shared equality on which her life with Admiral Croft is based. But here too the naval milieu is suggestive. Indeed even the critic who sees *Persuasion* as a radically optimistic change from Austen's earlier pessimism concedes that the humane relationships of the novel are presented in relation to the other-worldly image of the sea.[6] That other-worldliness reinforces the impression that Austen perceives the humane liberalism of the naval couples as the reflection of that liberating experience which is represented by their removal from a society of land-locked conventions. By comparison, the world of Mansfield Park receives a breath of fresh air with the visit of William Price, and in a more permanent sense it receives a new spirit in the marriage of his sister Fanny, who, significantly, is the one who displays an exceptional ability to graduate from the limiting conventions of her background to an unassuming but undeniably strong individualism.

In light of that tension which we have already noted in the *Letters*, between Austen's idealistic and realistic perception of marriage, it is significant that she invests the truly humane relationships of *Persuasion* with an other-worldliness that complements the exceptional nature of individual maturation in her world. For in implying that the really fulfilling and the truly humane are rare and improbable experiences Austen underscores her essentially bleak vision of the individual and society. That bleakness is manifest in her correspondence as well as her fiction. Viewed in relation to her novels the wit which repeatedly crucifies her acquaintance in the *Letters* is more than a species of gossipy small-talk. It also reflects a deep-seated impatience with individual silliness and with defective social institutions around her. On a similar basis the few good marriages in the novels and the exceptional individuals who make them possible do little to obscure or soften the harsh images of marriage and motherhood in the works. In the case of motherhood Mrs Bennet is of course the most arresting example of her kind in the novels. The connection between her inadequacies as mother and the failings of her younger daughters are clear enough. And Austen's unsparing attention to the logic of her fictive realism leaves us no assurances that Mrs Bennet is capable of change: 'Happy for all her maternal feelings was the day on which Mrs. Bennet got rid of her two most deserving daughters. ... I wish I could say, for the sake of her family, that the accomplishment of her earnest desire in the establishment of so many of her children, produced so happy an effect as to make her a sensible, amiable, well-informed woman for the rest of her life' (*P&P*, p. 385). These rather obvious elaborations on Mrs Bennet's failings as a mother do have the important effect of underlining Austen's perception of maternal failures as an extension of the inadequacies of the woman's education and individual development. Mrs Bennet and her kind are foolish, disagreeable, and ill-informed women, the kind of women who prompt Mary Wollstonecraft, for one, to decry the limited education of women and its cramping effects on the very roles (of wife and mother) that that education supposedly prepares them for: 'Women are told from their infancy, and taught by the example of their mothers, that a little knowledge of human weakness, justly termed cunning, softness of temper, *outward* obedience, and a scrupulous attention to a puerile kind of propriety, will obtain for them the protection of man' (*Rights of Woman*, p. 49). Women of 'mean understanding' and 'uncertain' temper, such as Mrs Bennet, are therefore incapable of 'maternal feelings' in any sense except as a narrowly egocentric self-indulgence. The child is really an object to be displayed, as in the case of the insipid Lady Middleton's children. Or, as with 'poor little Harry' in *Sense and Sensibility*, Fanny Dashwood's maternal solicitude is merely a thin disguise for a selfish materialism – in this case her determination to persuade the acquiescent John Dashwood against providing the older Mrs Dashwood with an annuity. And to return to Mrs Bennet and *her* maternal 'feelings', it is clear that the emotions which she feels have little to do with a selfless concern about the welfare of her daughters: for the highly suggestive language with which Austen describes those feelings (Mrs Bennet 'got rid' of her two 'most deserving' daughters) pinpoints the very narrow selfishness and insensitivity to the worth of others which invariably motivate her. She is the businesswoman disposing of her two most 'deserving' (marketable) commodities in the business of marriage. The child is the mother's marketable object, or an object for self-gratifying display. And this kind of mother-child relationship may very well explain why there is so little of genuine feeling and solicitude for children on the part of mothers or on the part of those substitute mothers whose adoptive role is almost as full-time as that of a natural mother. Indeed it is significant that so many of Austen's fictional mothers are associated with distorted or atrophied 'feelings' as mothers. Lady Bertram is the very epitome of a self-indulgent laziness that is incapable of any real solicitude for anyone, including her children. These mothers are all characterised by a selfishness (amounting to megalomania in the case of Mrs Ferrars) which is the very antithesis of maternal solicitude, but which has actually been encouraged by prevailing notions about the proper education of future wives and mothers. Motherhood, like marriage, is an extension of a deep-rooted and *continuing* value system geared to the production of silly, selfish creatures rather than rational women. To return to Mary Wollstonecraft – 'have women, who have early imbibed notions of passive obedience, sufficient character to manage a family or educate children?' (*Rights of Woman*, p. 69). Answering her own question, she observes, "To be a good mother – a woman must have sense, and that independence of mind which few women possess who are taught to depend entirely on their husbands. Meek wives are, in general, foolish mothers' (p. 227).

There seems no basis in either the fiction or the correspondence for assuming that Austen has any significant faith in the human capacity for a radical and widespread transformation of individuals and social institutions. The problem has been that her bleak moral vision is often distorted by our understandable but usually exclusive preoccupation with her comic tone and techniques. Her well known criticism of the 'light, and bright, and sparkling' tone of *Pride and Prejudice* is perhaps more than a playful jibe at popular novelists who pad out their narratives with 'solemn specious nonsense' (*Letters*, p. 299). It perhaps reflects the perfectionist's real concern about a possible discrepancy between her playful style and the hard realism, which, after all, does emphasise the continuity of defective norms in the persons of Lady Catherine, Wickham, Collins, and most poignantly, in the marriage of Mr and Mrs Bennet. Conversely, the controversial mood of *Mansfield Park* may seem less uncharacteristic than it has to most readers if its sombre quality were perceived as a reflection of the rather grim image of human nature and social behaviour in Austen's fictive vision as a whole.

From this viewpoint connubial felicity and the social and individual improvement which it enshrines at the end of the novels seem to function more as an ironic counterpoint to the dominant social realities which persist in the marriage of the Willoughbys, the Wickhams, and the Eltons. The happily ideal marriage does not seem to represent a general transformation of society, or even any capacity for such transformation. It does not seem to herald the 'brave new world' of new marriages, new men, and of course, new women which a feminist critic finds in *Persuasion*, for example.[7] The exceptional nature of individual maturation in the novels seems to have ironic implications for the happy marriage itself. The feminist idealism which may be inferred from such personal growth is integrated with the kind of satiric realism which offers no easy promises of the revolutionist's brave new world. And here she parts company with someone like Mary Wollstonecraft, whose equally realistic analysis of the woman's world is balanced by a strong faith in the future possibilities of a truly humanised society: 'as sound politics diffuse liberty, mankind, including woman, will become more wise and virtuous' (*Rights of Woman*, p. 73).

Consequently, it is important to note that the happy marriage of the hero and heroine is one of the comically self-conscious mechanics of Austen's happy endings.[8] In elaborating on the contrived inevitability of her happy endings Austen is able to emphasise in a comic way the superiority of her art to the more transparent artifices of popular fiction while at the same time conceding the essential artifices (including the happy ending) of her own fictive realism. But even more pertinent is the fact that this emphasis on the contrivance of the happy ending centres on the happy marriage. The 'tell-tale compression of the pages' which is to assure the anxious reader that the happy conclusion of *Northanger Abbey* is at hand also heralds the 'perfect felicity' of an 'early marriage' between Catherine and Henry (p. 250). Mrs Ferrars' hilarious ritual of execution-and-resuscitation finally culminates with the assurance that Edward will be happily, and prudently, married to Elinor – at the same time that it confirms to the end the continuity of Mrs Ferrars' tyranny and all that it represents (*S&S*, p. 373). Lady Catherine's autocratic and compulsive interference performs a similar service for Elizabeth and Darcy, and in the process ensures the connubial happy ending that Elizabeth playfully discusses with Darcy (*P&P*. p. 381). In *Emma* Mr Knightley's proposal and Emma's response are rendered with a comical *déjà vu* emphasis that sets the stage for the usual note of inevitability: 'What did she say? – Just what she ought, of course. A lady always does' (p. 431). In *Persuasion* the salute to imprudent love-matches sets the appropriate comic tone for the inevitable marriage plans of Anne and Wentworth. The decidedly grimmer tone of the ending of *Mansfield Park* is actually the converse rather than the exception in that it directly confronts the realities (including the sexual double standard that punishes Maria Rushworth but not Henry Crawford) which are usually detoured, but ironically implied, by the happy endings of the other novels.

It follows from all of this that the happy marriages with which the novels close are part of the idealistic vision which serves a moral function of its own while being simultaneously subjected to the novelist's satiric realism. The marriages celebrate the achievement of a moral and intellectual excellence which fulfils a moral ideal but which, for that very reason, is unreal – a felicitous contrivance by the novelist's ethical vision, her feminist value system, and her fictive art. Hence the very *unreality* of a happy marriage or of a truly humane motherhood becomes a satiric reflection on the very real limitations of society and individuals. To return to the dominant social symbol in *Persuasion*, the naval ambience represents the exceptional, a delightfully idyllic uprootedness which releases the individual from prevailing social inadequacies; but in the final analysis it is a satirically inverted mirror-image of the dominant reality. Of course her unrelenting attention to the logic of the real world does not undermine Austen's moral idealism on behalf of personal integrity and regarding the woman's individuality. For it is precisely this idealism which, in turn, sharpens her satiric perception of marriage, motherhood, and society as they really are in her world.

NOTES

1 Mona Wilson, *Jane Austen and Some Contemporaries* (London, 1938); Mark Schorer, 'Pride Unprejudiced', *Kenyon Review*, 18 (winter 1956) pp. 83, 85.

2 See, for example, E. Margaret Moore, 'Emma and Miss Bates: Early Experiences of Separation and the Theme of Dependency in Jane Austen's Novels', *Studies in English Literature*, 9 (autumn 1969) pp. 573–85; Helen Storm Corsa, 'A Fair but Frozen Maid: A Study of Jane Austen's *Emma*', *Literature and Psychology*, 19 (1969) pp. 101–23.

3 C. A. Linder, 'The Ideal of Marriage as Depicted in the Novels of Jane Austen and Charlotte Brontë', *Standpunte*, 24 (Aug 1971) pp. 20–30.

4 According to Patricia Meyer Spacks, for example, 'Marriage can be, and usually is, a particularly useful way of fulfilling the fundamental human need to discover and assert one's value'. *The Female Imagination* (New York, 1975) p. 117.

5 Compare Mary Wollstonecraft, *A Vindication of the Rights of Woman* (1792) Norton Library edition (New York, 1967) p. 81. In a similar vein Fanny Price's uniquely intense sense of integrity is complemented by her physical and social isolation at Mansfield Park. And as Patricia Spacks notes, Emma's way-

ward imagination actually distinguishes her from her more nondescript contemporaries and contributes eventually to her growth (*The Female Imagination*, pp. 124–5).

6 Nina Auerbach, 'O Brave New World: Evolution and Revolution in *Persuasion*', *ELH*, 39 (Mar 1972) p. 123.

7 Ibid., pp. 112–28.

8 Compare Lloyd W. Brown, *Bits of Ivory: Narrative Techniques in Jane Austen's Fiction* (Baton Rouge, La, 1973) pp. 222–35.

3 The Great Tradition Revisited

NORMAN PAGE

One of the most interesting unwritten books of our time was promised, or at least adumbrated, in the second sentence of F. R. Leavis's *The Great Tradition*.[1] I suppose some of us can still recall the *frisson* of astonishment with which, more than a quarter of a century ago, we read the opening sentence of that book – a sentence reminiscent in its resonant, uncompromising simplicity of the opening of Genesis:

> The great English novelists are Jane Austen, George Eliot, Henry James and Joseph Conrad . . .

The sentence which follows the one I have quoted announces the scope of the book as being limited to the last three of this improbable quartet (or such it certainly seemed in the forties); and adds, by way of explanation, that 'Jane Austen, for special reasons, needs to be studied at considerable length'. To which we may retort, with Byron, 'I wish he would explain his explanation'; for those 'special reasons' were not divulged, and I am perhaps not the only reader, then and now, to find them less than self-evident. Nor has that study of Jane Austen 'at considerable length' ever appeared, either from Dr Leavis's pen or from that of Mrs Leavis, who in 1948 already had a reputation as an Austen scholar on the strength of a group of important articles published in *Scrutiny*. But some light is thrown on this question of the book that never was by a letter contributed by Mrs Leavis to the *Times Literary Supplement* at almost exactly the time *The Great Tradition* was published – a letter which suggests that she had, by mutual agreement, pre-empted Jane Austen:

> I should long ago have finished the book of which the articles form part if it had been possible to make use of the corroborative evidence that I believe may be found in the missing-link stories

in Jane Austen's unpublished manuscript collection, *Volume the
Third*, which apparently no one outside the Austen-Leigh family
but Dr. Chapman has ever seen.[2]

Dr Chapman did in fact publish *Volume the Third* three years later;
but Mrs Leavis's book is still awaited. Perhaps the 'corroborative
evidence' which was to demonstrate the continuity of Jane Austen's
literary career turned out not to be there after all. Be that as it may,
and for whatever reason, Dr Leavis's attitude to Jane Austen in
The Great Tradition is one of curious and voluntary self-denial: we
are told plainly that she is the first great English novelist, but his
scattered references to her amount to the equivalent of no more
than a couple of pages. During the twenty years or so which followed
The Great Tradition, we had from Leavis a full-length study of
D. H. Lawrence (1955), as well as the Leavises' joint study, *Dickens
the Novelist* (1970) – two books which, together with a handful of
shorter pieces, serve both to supplement and to qualify the claims
and arguments advanced in the 1948 volume. In these later critical
writings, the position of Jane Austen is neither explicitly defended
nor seriously challenged. There is, perhaps, the smallest of straws
in the wind in Mrs Leavis's observation (in one of her Dickens
essays) that Jane Austen lacks imaginative sympathy[3] – but that is
hardly substantial enough for even the most desperate historian of
critical trends to clutch at.

Jane Austen's place in the 'great tradition' remains, then, somewhat obscure: asserted in general terms but never demonstrated
with the kind of particularity we associate with Leavis's characteristic critical method. But, if obscure, her place is also a uniquely
prominent one; and it seems worth enquiring by virtue of what
qualities her novels may be supposed to have earned this ranking;
what is the nature of the tradition of which she is not only a member
but, according to Leavis, the inaugurator; and, more especially,
what kind of relationship she enjoys to the later members of the
tradition. These seem to me to be fruitful questions for the literary
historian as well as the critic, for the student of Jane Austen in
particular and the English novel in general. I am not unmindful of
the objections that can be levelled against criticism of criticism: the
critic's critic, like the gentleman's gentleman, occupies a somewhat
ambiguous position in the hierarchy; but there is surely a sound case
to be made for attempting to elucidate the judgements of a major
critic on a major novelist.

If we begin by asking: what, for Leavis, is the nature of the 'great tradition', we shall find the question harder to answer than to ask. Some of those who reviewed the book when it first appeared regarded the large claims of its title as misleading and unfortunate. W. W. Robson, for instance, while praising Leavis's particular analyses, criticised 'the vagueness of the underlying critical concepts'; and George Orwell observed (in the *Observer*), 'Just where the "tradition" comes in it is not easy to say'.[4] Part of the answer seems to be that the emphasis should fall on the adjective rather than the noun: Leavis is concerned with a tradition of greatness, rather than major instances of demonstrable influence and indebtedness. And certainly, if we insist on understanding *tradition* in its etymological sense, as a 'handing over' of distinctive and definable preoccupations and achievements, or in the sense in which literary historians normally employ the term (in speaking, for instance, of the Chaucerian tradition, or of what Leavis himself in another book calls the Augustan tradition of verse), then we are quickly in trouble. Already in the 1948 book Jane Austen is to be found consorting with strange bedfellows (if that indelicate expression may be excused): what, we may wonder, are Conrad and Lawrence up to in her company, and she in theirs? Confusion is compounded when we check the later and fuller exemplifications of the tradition, such as that in the study of Lawrence, where Leavis refers to 'the work of the great novelists from Jane Austen to Lawrence', and cites by way of further definition 'Hawthorne, Dickens, George Eliot, Henry James, Melville, Mark Twain, Conrad'. (This same muster-roll had appeared somewhat earlier, by the way, in another context, and with the omission of Mark Twain's name.)[5] There is evidently an American great tradition in the nineteenth century as well as an English one; or is it all one tradition of the novel written in English? It is tempting to settle the question by concluding that these are, for Leavis, no more than what the Victorians would have called the 'best authors' – his personal syllabus for a 'great books' course. Such was the conclusion of another of the early reviewers of *The Great Tradition*, who expressed considerable scepticism about the claims of its title: 'the idea [of a tradition]', wrote an anonymous critic in the *Listener*, 'is little more than a spurious, inserted *leitmotiv* ... vamped up into an overture before the real business begins'.[6] This won't quite do, however; for there clearly *are*, among some of the writers in the list I have quoted, important lines of influence discernible, 'traditions' of relationships based on the common

pursuit of fictional aims, and manifested both by general indebtedness and by similarities deriving from specific, conscious knowledge.
Dickens was an important influence on Conrad; George Eliot knew
her Jane Austen, and was in turn thoroughly known by Henry
James; Lawrence wrote about the American novelists, for example;
but the task of defining a single tradition linking Austen with
Melville and James with Lawrence (to combine and permute no
further) seems likely to baffle the most resolute and ruthless critical
ingenuity.

And yet we cannot altogether discard the etymological or (as it
were) traditional meaning of *tradition*; and it is worth noting that
Leavis himself is far from indifferent to, or unobservant of, this kind
of direct relationship locally manifested. He discerns in James's *The
Europeans*, for instance, the presence of Jane Austen; he stresses
the pressure of Dickensian models in *The Secret Agent*; he shows
how much *The Portrait of a Lady* owes to *Daniel Deronda*; he cites
Hawthorne as an influence on both George Eliot and Henry James.
It is evident, though, that for Leavis this is not the whole truth
about tradition in the novel, or even the most important part of it:
the notes-and-queries approach of tracing echoes and allusions,
borrowings and parallels, interests him, I think, only as helping to
reinforce and exemplify his main contentions. And, as he makes
clear, indebtedness is not necessarily a matter of similarity: indeed,
in his words, 'the profoundest kind of influence [is] not manifested
in likeness' (p. 10); while 'influence' in the restricted sense of
imitation can be positively baleful, as in some of the manifestations
of the Dickensian tradition in later Victorian novelists. What a
writer of fiction gains from his significant predecessors seems to be
less a matter of 'models' than of an enlarged and enriched sense of
the possibilities of the medium. *Mansfield Park* is the first modern
novel, as Mrs Leavis among others has claimed, not because Fanny
Price is a prototype of the nineteenth-century heroine but because
the novel is used to probe the kind of questions that continued to
interest George Eliot, Henry James, and other novelists for at least
a hundred years after Jane Austen's death.

Although Leavis says so little that is explicitly related to Jane
Austen, we can gather some sense of the claims he makes for her by
looking at the company she keeps in his criticism, and the contexts
in which her name is, however briefly, invoked. Let me quote from
a passage in which he proposes a relationship between *The
Europeans* and the later novels of Jane Austen. He notes that, while

James's novel can be read 'straightforwardly as novel of manners and social comedy', it is also 'rich ... in symbolic and poetic interest', and possesses a 'deep and close organization as fable and dramatic poem'. These observations both describe James's novel and instruct us how to read Jane Austen, for they lead straight into the suggestion that 'in *The Europeans* it is pretty clearly from Jane Austen that James descends; what he offers is a development in the line of *Emma* and *Persuasion*'.[7] (That link between the late Austen and the early James is something I want to return to later.) Again, Leavis elsewhere praises *The Portrait of a Lady* in terms that are wholly applicable to Jane Austen's novels, and contrives simultaneously to take a sideswipe at those Victorian novelists he regards as overrated: 'it offers no largesse of irrelevant "life"; its vitality is wholly that of art'; it is tightly organised and 'all intensely significant' (p. 152). It is significant, too, that the passage I have quoted from continues with contrasting references to, on the one hand, 'Trollope, Mrs. Gaskell, and the rest' – the not-so-great tradition, as it were – and also to Jane Austen and George Eliot, whose general recognition as classics has, he argues, obscured their real claims to distinction.

The fullest statement concerning Jane Austen in *The Great Tradition* (and even that amounts to no more than a few lines) places the emphasis firmly on her 'intense moral interest ... in life' (p. 7) – an interest that, as Leavis sees it, involves the impersonalisation of personal problems and their embodiment in an appropriate form. Her title as 'the inaugurator of the great tradition' (p. 7) is substantiated by two important, though not equally important, qualities: not only does she manifest an 'intense moral preoccupation' (p. 7) which is the distinguishing mark of novelists in the tradition; she also evinces a mature concern with form and technique (he speaks, for instance, of the 'perfection of form' [p. 8] to be found in *Emma*). These are, respectively, the major and minor bases of her greatness: Leavis has no time for the appreciation of 'form' as a discrete element – such gross critical error is liable to evoke scornful references to Bloomsbury. The economy, selection and control to be found in Jane Austen's fiction are a function of her 'marked moral intensity': her technique, with all its accomplishments and innovations, is a necessary formal embodiment of concerns which lie beneath and beyond aesthetics.

The other novelists of the great tradition claim their places therein by virtue of sharing her profound interest in the problems of living.

The question remains: do they share anything else? If not, then we are driven back to the unexciting possibility mooted earlier that the so-called 'tradition' involves nothing more than a shared but widely different greatness, a general community of excellence. Leavis's own conception of the tradition certainly seems to contain elements of inconsistency.[8] He is capable of stating roundly, near the beginning of his book, that he is 'not concerned to establish *indebtedness*' (p. 15); but he also in other places stresses the historical significance of Jane Austen, who 'creates the tradition we see leading down to her' and is 'herself a major fact in the background of other great writers' (p. 5). Almost in spite of himself, Leavis offers us a persuasive view of Jane as Janus, looking both ways down the vistas of the English novel from her vantage-point between the eighteenth century and the Victorians. For to say that she is a 'major fact in the background of other great writers' (and that observation may serve as a text for the remainder of this paper) can only mean that, consciously or unconsciously, directly or indirectly, they learned something of importance from her: they do not simply share a common excellence, but possess qualities in common with her and with others which we ought to be able to identify and locate in their work, and to separate from those elements derived from other sources.

Leavis himself undertakes this comparative task only fitfully: it is perhaps relevant to remind ourselves that much of the book first appeared in the form of separate essays on individual authors, and the cross-stitching was somewhat perfunctorily carried out, so that it retains something of its piecemeal origins. When he does venture upon the demonstration of relationships, he is at his most vulnerable, and his discovery of his own vulnerability seems to be confessed by certain revisions made (though without appropriate indications for the most part) in later versions of the book.[9] These revisions embody one or two significant shifts of judgement as well as several silent adjustments in arguments which turn out to have been based on error. I can best illustrate them, and at the same time suggest that it is possible to venture further than Leavis does in tracing lines of influence, by looking at what he says about Jane Austen's relationship first to George Eliot, and then to Henry James.

'It is not for nothing that George Eliot admired [Jane Austen's] work profoundly, and wrote one of the earliest appreciations of it to be published.' Thus Leavis in 1948 (p. 9). But as he should have known, and as Joseph Cady and Ian Watt have pointed out in their lively round-up of Austen critics,[10] George Eliot didn't write that appreciation, which is by Lewes; and the sentence I have quoted has now been revised to read: 'There is evidence enough that George Eliot admired her work profoundly.'[11] If the letter of Leavis's scholarship was faulty, however, there was nothing wrong with the spirit of his earlier claim: there is indeed 'evidence enough' of a profound admiration, manifesting itself both locally and pervasively, in specific borrowings and in a larger indebtedness. As so often, the contemporary reception points the way for us quite clearly: it is striking to note how readily and frequently Jane Austen's name comes to mind for George Eliot's first readers and critics, many of whom turn naturally to her work for comparisons in their attempts to define and evaluate what George Eliot was doing. E. S. Dallas, reviewing *Felix Holt* in *The Times*, finds her lacking in Jane Austen's narrative skill, partly because she is dealing with more ambitious and more complex themes. In somewhat similar vein we have W. H. Mallock's remark in the *Edinburgh Review* that 'she might have been a second Miss Austen': like Dallas, Mallock saw George Eliot as refusing to pay the necessary price of 'perfect art' in the coin of self-imposed limitations. And Henry James himself, in his important review of *Middlemarch*, described Celia Brooke as 'as pretty a fool as any of Miss Austen's'. Nor is it surprising to find a mention of Jane Austen in the letter Lewes wrote to John Blackwood to accompany the manuscript of *Scenes of Clerical Life*; and when Lewes stresses the limitations of Jane Austen in his substantial essay on her work, he is surely, without naming names, making an implicit comparison with George Eliot in suggesting of the earlier novelist that 'she never stirs the deeper emotions, . . . she never fills the soul with a noble aspiration, or brightens it with a fine idea'.[12] The example of Jane Austen was certainly before George Eliot when she made her early attempts at fiction: we know from their letters that she and Lewes read *Emma* and two or three of her other novels aloud at the time 'Janet's Repentance' was written;[13] and while that story could not have been written by Jane Austen, we can see her influence in the presentation of a strictly limited but varied society, the close-up view of mildly idiosyncratic speech and behaviour, and especially in the brilliant comedy of the tea-table gathering in the third chapter. That 'confidence in the significance of the quotidian' which David Lodge has detected in the early George Eliot is the very basis of Jane Austen's art, which was in turn praised by a Victorian critic for its mastery over 'the region of commonplace'.[14]

The other end of George Eliot's career offers a more substantial example of influence, and *Daniel Deronda* is doubly significant for my purposes because it links Jane Austen through George Eliot with Henry James, who wrote at length about this novel when it appeared, and later described himself (in *The Middle Years*) as 'even a very Derondist of Derondists'.[15] Once again, we have a record of Jane Austen being read aloud in the Lewes *ménage* whilst the novel was being written. *Middlemarch* had opened with a variation on a theme already familiar from *Emma:* the folly of which the clever are especially capable ('Miss Brooke,' we read, 'was certainly very naive with all her alleged cleverness'); and in the contrasting use of the two sisters, *Middlemarch* had also echoed a thematic device of *Sense and Sensibility. Daniel Deronda,* though it eventually moves in very different directions, takes as its starting-point a situation which recalls certain elements, and even certain episodes, in other Austen novels. Early in the book we find a parallel, and perhaps even a conscious allusion, to *Pride and Prejudice.* Just as the earlier novel opens with the news 'that Netherfield Park is let at last' to a wealthy young bachelor, in *Deronda* we find a sense of expectation created by the news that Diplow Hall is to be occupied by a young man of ample fortune and aristocratic hopes. In the narrator's comment that 'Some readers of this history will doubtless regard it as incredible that people should construct matrimonial prospects on the mere report that a bachelor of good fortune and possibilities was coming within reach ...' (*Daniel Deronda,* Chapter 9) we may be reminded of the celebrated opening of *Pride and Prejudice;* and the small-minded schemings of Gwendolen's mother, and the ironic treatment she receives, strongly recall the presentation of Mrs Bennet. Other elements in the initial situations are closer to those of *Mansfield Park:* in both novels, an impoverished wife's sister's family is taken under the wing of a prosperous brother-in-law, after some preliminary misgivings. The Rev. Gascoigne is anxious about his sons ('I hope they will not be falling in love with Gwendolen,' he remarks), and his anxiety exactly parallels that of Sir Thomas Bertram; whilst the reassurance he receives that 'cousins will not fall in love' is a less emphatic version of Mrs Norris's claim: 'It is morally impossible. I never knew an instance of it.' Except in situation, it is true, Gwendolen Harleth is no Fanny Price: she is only too eager to act in 'charades or theatrical pieces, occasions which she meant to bring about by force of will or contrivance'; and in her self-seeking wilfulness, she is closer to Mary Crawford.

One might continue the enumeration of echoes and parallels; but it needs to be stressed that there is, of course, a lot in George Eliot's last novel which *doesn't* derive from Jane Austen, and that the book has virtues and defects which would have been alike beyond her. I don't wish to appear to exaggerate either the extent or the nature of George Eliot's debt to Jane Austen. Tracing influences and establishing parallels is liable to induce a curious variety of optical defect, whereby some areas in the field of vision become highly magnified whilst others diminish or vanish. The central achievement of George Eliot, and what we may call her characteristic tone or note, derive from the integration of a superb intelligence, wide and deep learning, and a long and strenuous experience of the problems of living; and it would be foolish to claim that she owes this quality to Jane Austen or to any other writer, or that Jane Austen can precisely match this extraordinary blend of qualifications. On the other hand, although some of the developments in George Eliot's fiction are indebted to nothing but her own genius, Jane Austen seems to have provided her with a point of departure: it is notable that, beginning to write fiction in the late fifties, she should have sought a model not in Dickens or any other contemporary novelist, but – like Mrs Gaskell a decade earlier – should have gone back (as she goes back in the period setting of so many of her books) to an earlier writer. It may be more than a coincidence, of course, that she went back to a novelist of her own sex; but one can only applaud and endorse Leavis's comment that 'except for Jane Austen there was no novelist to learn from – none whose work had any bearing on her own essential problems as a novelist' (p. 10).

Once the necessary caveats have been entered, it has to be said that *Daniel Deronda* bears many of the hall-marks of a tradition for which Jane Austen seems to be largely responsible, if not the only begetter. The ironic comedy and commentary (witness the remark, very much in Jane Austen's vein, that Gwendolen's mother's conversation derived from little more than the possession of 'the faculty of speech and the not knowing what to do with it'); the presentation of a heroine confronting the world, and discovering the unsoundness of her judgements and the impracticability of her ambitions; above all the pervasive assumption that conduct matters and that behaviour in even the most trivial circumstances can be of supreme significance – these qualities irresistibly recall Jane Austen's mode of story-telling and her conception of the function of the novel. At the beginning of *Daniel Deronda*, we find Gwendolen referring to her sister in a way that tells us more about the speaker than pertains to the single occasion or that one relationship: she complains of having to give her sister lessons, saying that

'It bores me to death, she is so slow. . . . It would be much better for her to be ignorant, mamma: it is her *rôle*, she would do it well.'
'That is a hard thing to say of your poor sister, Gwendolen. . . .'
'I don't see why it is hard to call things by their right names, and put them in their proper places . . .' (Chapter 3).

These, we feel, are the very tones Mary Crawford might have used on such an occasion – and that Elizabeth Bennet might have felt like using but would not have permitted herself.

To the qualities I have proposed as constituting Jane Austen's contribution to the art of George Eliot and the nineteenth-century tradition, I would add the fashioning of a language (most evidently in *Persuasion*) to trace and describe states of mind and feeling. Jane Austen is as aware as Virginia Woolf that life is made up not only of actions and speeches but of what she calls, in two different passages in *Emma*, 'zigzags of emotion' and 'the wonderful velocity of thought'. Several critics have noted the parallel between George Eliot's analysis, in the twentieth chapter of *Middlemarch*, of Dorothea's state of mind during her Roman honeymoon, and the famous forty-second chapter of *The Portrait of a Lady*; but we surely find a prototype for both of these in that magnificent section near the end of *Emma* which follows the heroine's discovery 'that Mr. Knightley must marry no one but herself!' If *Mansfield Park* is the first modern novel, then *Emma* is surely the second. Its subject is the relationship between the inner and outer lives, its business to analyse and dramatise the workings of the mind in relation to conduct; and, apart from the moral interest of the enterprise, its technical originality is astonishing. Henry James can scarcely keep the note of self-congratulation out of his voice when, in his preface to *The Portrait of a Lady*, he states the problem from which he started as one of endowing 'the mere slim shade of an intelligent but presumptuous girl . . . with the high attributes of a Subject'; but Jane Austen had tackled precisely that problem, and solved it triumphantly, seventy years earlier.

If I seem to have slipped into speaking of James's relationship to Jane Austen, that is not altogether accidental, and is certainly appropriate. Joseph Cady and Ian Watt, in the survey of Austen criticism I have already mentioned, again take Leavis to task for his claim that 'Henry James ... was a great admirer of Jane Austen' (p. 10), pointing out that James accords her unfavourable mention in two of his essays. But it ought to be said (and here I am criticising the critic's critics) that the earlier of these essays dates from as late as 1902, and that long before this date all of James's fiction that Leavis regards as his finest was written: so that the attempt to weaken Leavis's case need not be taken very seriously. It is true that James's earlier references to Jane Austen are fairly sparse; we ought not perhaps to hold against him too severely his conventionally inadequate characterisation of her, in a review written when he was only twenty-two,[16] as the inventor of 'the novel of domestic tranquillity'. What is surely more significant is that, reading the stories and novels of James up to *The Portrait of a Lady*, one is continually reminded of Jane Austen by his recurring themes and situations, and even by the language and tone of his dialogue and commentary. Marrying and giving in marriage, and the economic implications and consequences of these ever-interesting activities, are as much a preoccupation in James's early fiction as in Austen's novels. Newman in *The American* is a single man of good fortune in want of a wife; and the fortune-hunter in *Washington Square* might have given Mr Elton a few points. A favourite early-Jamesian gambit is to create problems for his characters through inequality of wealth: repeatedly the heroine is loved by a poor man, or some other fiscal hazard is encountered; whilst his early narrators are apt to speak of romance and finance in the same breath, and even to use monetary metaphors in describing the human heart, in a manner that recalls the first page of *Mansfield Park* and many a similar passage. A heroine of one early story is 'twenty-five years of age, beautiful, accomplished and conscious of good investments'; the hero of another is 'rich in ... his little capital of uninvested affections.' In conveying such sentiments, Henry James can even be led to imitate Jane Austen's diction and syntax to a degree that verges on pastiche. In the fourth story he ever published ('A Day of Days'), for instance, he writes: 'She was ... mistress of a very pretty little fortune, and was accounted clever without detriment to her amiability, and amiable without detriment to her wit'[17] – in which language and tone seem consciously to look back to Regency England from the New England of 1866. His insistence (in a letter to Howells) that 'it takes an old civilization to set a novelist in motion' shows the need he felt to attach himself to the English tradition; and when he continues in the same letter, 'It is on manners, customs, usages, habits, forms, upon all these things matured and established, that a novelist lives – they are the very stuff his work is made of',[18] we have a specification for the art of the novel that, among James's predecessors, is nowhere more closely met than in the work of Jane Austen. The twentieth-century revaluation of Jane Austen was partly initiated by critics schooled in the Jamesian house of fiction; and for the present-day reader, *Emma* and *The Ambassadors* are closer to each other than either is to most of the novels that fall chronologically between them.

Structurally, too, the kind of novel James began by writing resembles those of Jane Austen more closely than anything else which was available to him. The slight edifice of his very first novel, *Watch and Ward*, is built around the Austenite formula of 'three or four families' – in this case, in upper-class Boston. This short novel presents a closely-observed society and uses dialogue to anatomise the petty dishonesties and transparent pretences of the morally weak. Professor Edel has noted the appearance in *Watch and Ward* of certain male character-types which 'reappear, with modifications, in *The Portrait of a Lady* and *The Wings of the Dove*', and which he designates 'the Loyal, the Strong and the Cunning'. He also observes in passing that there are moments at which this early novel 'might have come from the pen of a more amateurish Jane Austen';[19] he might, though, have gone a little further and pointed out that these character-types are also prominent in her novels. In the company of Roger Lawrence and Ralph Touchett, for instance, we might place Edmund Bertram, Edward Ferrars, and George Knightley; while Fenton and Osmond are spiritual younger brothers to Willoughby, Frank Churchill and Henry Crawford.

In much of this early fiction, James's narrative thread is spun remarkably thin, and the comments of his early critics often resemble the stock judgement on Jane Austen's novels that nothing happens at great length. 'There is hardly any plot at all . . . – perhaps sufficient, but barely sufficient, for threading together some admirably dramatic and highly humorous conversation' – thus the *Spectator* on *The Europeans*. 'No one does anything; . . . what is there, then? There is contrast of character, and conversation' was an American reviewer's verdict on the same novel. And Richard Grant White, still on *The Europeans*, remarks more succinctly of its characters that 'their sayings are many and their doings few.'[20] Like Jane Austen, James pursues his narrative leisurely but purposefully by presenting a series of formal and semi-formal social occasions –

a ball in *The American*, an engagement-party in *Washington Square*, visits and interviews conducted with a decorum which seems little more relaxed than in the England of half a century earlier. And, as Professor Edel has pointed out, the centre of James's stage, at any rate from *Confidence* (1879) onwards, is occupied by his heroines:[21] he has given us a series of 'studies of the female sensibility', of those 'frail vessels' (to borrow the phrase which James adapted from George Eliot) who are also at the centre of Jane Austen's world. If we ask what happens in these novels, the answer is that people talk; and some of the most momentous 'events' are the climaxes of conversation, the unexpected revelations and discoveries and eruptions of feeling which are liable to punctuate even the most commonplace of dialogues. The last five chapters of *The Portrait of a Lady* provide a cluster of examples, as Isabel Archer, leaving her husband in Italy for Ralph's deathbed, interviews in turn nearly every one of the novel's major characters. Although there is a journey and a death in these pages, the real *events* lie not in action but in the drama of verbal communication. James, like Austen, offers us a world in which the first requirement of a character is that he be articulate (again, the closing section of *Emma* comes to mind); both novelists express implicitly their faith in the possibility and the value of discourse.

Leavis's claim in *The Great Tradition* is that, in *The Portrait of a Lady*, James is heavily indebted to *Daniel Deronda*; but Professor Edel, anxious to defend James against the charge of derivativeness, insists that the themes of the *Portrait* can be found in his earlier, pre-*Deronda* fiction, and that George Eliot's novel 'fell on ground already fertile.'[22] My own contribution to this debate would be to suggest the possibility that both novels owe something to a common source in Jane Austen: if Isabel Archer and Gwendolen Harleth are transatlantic cousins, they are surely both in a direct line of descent from Emma Woodhouse. (Is it perhaps more than a coincidence that the name of Emma's sister is Isabella?) James's account of his method, in the preface to which I have already referred, is worth quoting from, even at some length, at this point:

'Place the centre of the subject in the young woman's own consciousness,' I said to myself, 'and you get as interesting and as beautiful a difficulty as you could wish. Stick to *that* – for the centre; put the heaviest weight into *that* scale, which will be so largely the scale of her relation to herself. Make her only interested enough, at the same time, in the things that are not herself, and this relation needn't fear to be too limited. Place meanwhile in the other scale the lighter weight (which is usually the one that tips the balance of interest): press least hard, in short, on the consciousness of your heroine's satellites, especially the male; make it an interest contributive only to the greater one ...'

The whole passage is of the greatest interest, and seems to me to be an extraordinarily accurate account of what Jane Austen is doing in *Emma*. The similiarity between the two novels wholly justifies Professor Arnold Kettle's making a unique exception of Jane Austen when he comments that 'the English novels which precede [*The Portrait of a Lady*] ... all seem a trifle crude.'²³ The similarity of starting-point in these novels, with their two 'presumptuous girls ... affront[ing] their destiny' (the phrases are James's) is very striking. Both girls are clever, but both possess qualities which render their cleverness a source of peril rather than satisfaction. Emma is an 'imaginist', and is spoilt and over-confident; and Isabel too has a 'strong' imagination, is subject to 'errors and delusions', is 'very liable to the sin of self-esteem' and 'in the habit of taking for granted, on scanty evidence, that she was right', and has 'an unquenchable desire to think well of herself' – I take all these phrases from the early chapters of James's novel, and all can be paralleled in the earlier book. Like Emma, Isabel confesses that 'If there's a thing in the world I'm fond of ... it's my personal independence.' And in James's diagnosis of Isabel's fateful immaturity – she has 'given undue encouragement to the faculty of seeing without judging' – we find a juxtaposition of ideas very characteristic of Jane Austen, and encountered, for instance, in *Mansfield Park*, when Fanny, more cautious and more self-aware than Emma, cannot feel sure that she is 'seeing clearly, and judging candidly'.

The crucial difference between the two novels is, of course, that James's is a tragedy – to use the word he applied to *Daniel Deronda*. The strictest of all Jane Austen's fictional conventions is that her heroines shall make their mistakes *before* marriage, thus preserving error as the stuff of comedy. (*Persuasion* is here, as in so many other respects, a partial though not a complete exception.) Jane Austen's notion of the place of marriage in fiction, at least for her protagonists, cannot accommodate post-marital unhappiness or recognition of error. Her commitment to the comic mode, at least up to and including *Emma*, means that her novels end at the point at which James's, like Eliot's, begin to deepen and intensify. Even in *Mansfield Park*, marital disaster is confined to a minor character and dealt with in summary fashion. But whereas Emma's premarital delusions are a laughing matter, Isabel's and Gwendolen's misjudgements are the bases of their unhappy marriages and of the extended exploration of the darker sides of human destiny.

George Eliot and Henry James: these are major halting-places, compulsory stops on the main line which connects Jane Austen with the twentieth century. There are several branch-lines, of varying degrees of importance: one, for example, leading to Trollope (and there is, incidentally, an interesting Victorian comparison between Jane Austen and Trollope, in an essay by Richard Holt Hutton);[24] another leading to Mrs Gaskell – but discussion of these is beyond the scope of the present essay. I should like to make an exception, though, in favour of a twentieth-century novelist who secures no place in Leavis's tradition, but whose achievement, as reckoned by some other critics, makes his debt to Jane Austen a matter of more than trivial interest. E. M. Forster received only the most cursory attention in the 1948 book (pp. 62–3), where his relationship to Jane Austen by way of George Eliot is noted but not discussed; but we can turn to a fine essay Leavis first published in *Scrutiny* in 1938 and reprinted in *The Common Pursuit* (1952); and the required link is made for us by finding Jane Austen's name, appropriately, on its very first page. Forster's use of comedy, Leavis argues, suggests comparisons with Jane Austen; on the other hand, there is in his work a 'poetic ambition' and 'a radical dissatisfaction with civilization' which have no counterparts in her novels. This seems to me an only partially correct, and certainly not an exhaustive, account of the relationship between these two authors. If Jane Austen does not express a 'dissatisfaction' with civilisation, she surely conveys, notably in *Mansfield Park*, a perceptive and even prophetic criticism of it; and Professor Whalley's essay in this collection may encourage us to disagree with Leavis on her lack of 'poetic ambition'. As we take a comparative glance at Austen and Forster, the century which separates them seems to shrink: at least superficially, these two celibate chroniclers of domestic experience in the home counties have much in common. Living outwardly uneventful lives, but both of them devoted correspondents and with strong family attachments; keenly observant of the niceties, and especially the minor betrayals, of speech and manners; with a reputation resting in each case on six short novels in which comedy and irony are the instruments of serious moral purpose, but which seem by their self-imposed limitations and strict conventions to invite critical undervaluation – no wonder one reviewer dubbed Forster's 'a twentieth-century Miss Austen', and another 'a comic genius of Austenite magnitude.' Sometimes critical judgements seem almost interchangeable, so that Lionel Trilling's reference to Forster's 'unremitting concern with moral realism' can serve also as a cogent statement of Jane Austen's strength.[25] As for Forster's declared estimate of her work, we have it both in *Aspects of the Novel* and, more informally, in *Abinger Harvest*, in a passage whose self-directed irony seems to warn us not to take it quite at face-value: I am thinking of Forster's account of himself as an arch-Austenite, 'slightly imbecile' about her, reading and re-reading with 'the mouth open and the mind closed'.[26] We ought not to make the mistake of treating such a passage with the kind of misplaced solemnity that has been accorded to some of Jane Austen's own *obiter dicta* – for example, that all-too-extensively invoked 'little bit of ivory'. To be taken more seriously is Forster's later and soberer statement (in a 1952 interview) that from Jane Austen he learned 'the possibilities of domestic humor'.[27]

Did he learn anything else from her? A partial answer may be found by putting together two novels in each of which a house provides the title and plays an important role. In *Mansfield Park* and *Howards End*, what Yeats calls 'one dear perpetual place' is both a focus of action and a bastion of values: and in each book, there is an unresolved problem arising from the imperfect identification of the human representatives with the houses to which they belong. Neither Sir Thomas Bertram nor Mrs Wilcox seems as impressive or as admirable as the moral and spiritual qualities which they and their homes seem intended to embody. But both novelists believe that the moral life is of overwhelming importance and fascination; and Forster seems to have resembled Jane Austen in the precocity and assurance with which he tackled moral issues and made moral judgements. His early fiction shows a knowledge, or knowingness, concerning the possibilities and pitfalls of conduct and feeling which recalls Jane Austen. As his biographer has written, Forster's most characteristic trait

> was his passion for moralising. He was moralising busily when he was twenty; and he continued, without intermission, for the next seventy years. He plainly regarded it as the business of life; one was on earth to improve oneself and to improve others, and the path to this was moral generalisations.[28]

One example of such a generalisation is all I have time for. *Howards End* is a twentieth-century novel, doing for the internal combustion engine what *Dombey and Son* does for the railway; but there is, in its last chapter, an observation which seems to me to link Forster with Jane Austen. Margaret Schlegel speaks there of 'the craze for motion [which] has only set in during the last hundred years'. Exactly one hundred years before Forster's novel was written, Jane Austen had used a 'craze for motion' as a moral danger-signal, a symptom of radical unsoundness of values. Any character in her novels who indulges in purposeless travel, motivated by nothing more serious than the quest for novelty, lays himself open to suspicion. The restless movement of the Crawfords between North-amptonshire and London is set in contrast against the more purpose-ful journeyings in the same novel: Sir Thomas risking his life on the high seas, Fanny (who travels so little) making her voyage of discovery to Portsmouth, and her brother visiting her during his rare and precious leaves.

Forster paid a marvellous tribute to Lawrence when the latter died, but his own novels seem to belong to a different century from Lawrence's. He said what he wanted to say – and, as we now know, went on saying it at least until the late fifties – without calling upon the art of fiction to undergo formal revolutions; and in technique and tone his detailed documentation of a narrow social world is closer to Jane Austen than to any novelist of his own time or the generations which separate them. The ethical landscapes of North-amptonshire and Hertfordshire are not, of course, identical: they could hardly be that, not least because Forster's moral convictions have behind them the pressure of personal problems different from Jane Austen's; and once again it will not do to push the resemblances too hard. On another (though related) level, too, *Howards End* is a very different novel from *Mansfield Park*. In the ninety-six years which separate them, the English language had not stood still; and the eighteenth-century moral vocabulary which Jane Austen is able to employ with such firmness and precision is no longer available to Forster. An article published a few years ago in *Essays in Criticism*[29] analyses the language of Forster's novel and states the stylistic case against him with considerable relish: his taste for the pseudo-archaic, the debased literary, the cliché, the epigram and the self-consciously symbolic are flaws, though not, I think, disastrous ones. Where Jane Austen is able to use key-words capable of conveying ethical concepts with a strength that is traditional as well as personal, and of becoming further refined in meaning on successive appearances, Forster can merely repeat phrases: 'only connect', 'panic and emptiness', 'telegrams and anger', which seem little more than approximate gestures in a promising direction. What he cannot do through the language itself, he is driven, sometimes regrettably, to attempt through obtrusive epigrams and short interpolated essays.

It has become evident, I think, that the relationships I have described between Jane Austen and three novelists of the hundred years which followed her death are manifested on several levels. Local allusions and echoes abound. When Forster, for example, begins a chapter with the words, 'We are not concerned with the very poor. They are unthinkable, and only to be approached by the statistician or the poet' (*Howards End*, Chapter 6), it is not very far-fetched to suggest that his tone and manner are consciously modelled on another famous chapter-opening: 'Let other pens dwell on guilt and misery. I quit such odious subjects as soon as I can' (*MP*, p. 461) – a passage which, incidentally, is again invoked, for different purposes, in Virginia Woolf's *Orlando*. But resemblances of this kind, though suggestive, scarcely provide a solid enough foundation on which to construct the idea of a tradition. What is more significant, though less easy to point to in a text, is a shared notion among these authors of the purpose of the novel and of its relevance to the business of living, as well as a shared notion of the nature of the genre. And it is at this point that one must again confront the problem raised by the highly eclectic membership of Leavis's 'great tradition', especially as amplified by his post-1948 writings. It is tempting to suggest that, in the title of the original book, the indefinite should have been preferred to the definite article: if there is *a* great tradition which begins with Jane Austen, there is surely at least one other which begins elsewhere – with Shakespeare and the Romantic poets, perhaps – and which includes Dickens and other novelists whose fiction is radically different in kind.[30] To insist on accommodating the latter in the Austen tradition is surely to weaken the distinctive force of any account of that tradition. For in such an account the emphasis must surely fall on the overriding preoccupation with moral issues. If, like Forster, we 'read and re-read' Jane Austen in the late decades of the twentieth century, it is – not exclusively, of course, but very importantly – because she is the kind of novelist who ceaselessly calls into question our own behaviour and self-awareness: the six short novels, so much less demanding of house-room than the collected work of George Eliot or James, require us to examine with rigour and urgency our conduct and our conversation, and, as we live our lives, to ask ourselves, not without frequent discomfort, what Jane Austen would have found herself impelled to say about us.

NOTES

(This paper owes a good deal to conversations I have had with my colleague Professor Christopher Drummond.)

1 All references are to the original edition of *The Great Tradition* (London, 1948), unless otherwise stated.

2 *Times Literary Supplement*, 4 Dec 1948, p. 681.

3 F. R. Leavis and Q. D. Leavis, *Dickens the Novelist* (London, 1970) p. 123.

4 Robson's review appeared in the *Review of English Studies*, n.s., I (1950) p. 377; Orwell's in the *Observer* for 6 Feb 1949, p. 3.

5 F. R. Leavis, *D. H. Lawrence: Novelist* (London, 1955) p. 18. *Anna Karenina and Other Essays* (London, 1967) pp. 145–6.

6 *Listener*, xli (1949) p. 819.

7 *Anna Karenina and Other Essays*, p. 74.

8 And even, one might add, of tautology: '. . . by "great tradition" I mean the tradition to which what is great in English fiction belongs' (p. 7).

9 The numerous minor though significant revisions in later impressions of the book are a subject for a study in themselves. The textual history of *The Great Tradition* is somewhat obscure: for instance, the 1960 'fourth impression' is now described as a 'new edition'. See D. F. McKenzie and M-P. Allum, *F. R. Leavis: A Check-List 1924–1964* (London, 1966) p. 47.

10 Joseph Cady and Ian Watt, 'Jane Austen's Critics', *Critical Quarterly*, v (1963) p. 56. However, their statement that 'there seems to be no other evidence of George Eliot's admiration (or otherwise) for Jane Austen' can certainly be disputed. See, for example, note 13 below.

11 *The Great Tradition* (Harmondsworth, 1962) p. 18; and similarly in other recent editions.

12 The passages by Dallas, Mallock and James and the letter by Lewes are reprinted in *George Eliot: the Critical Heritage*, ed. David Carroll (London, 1971) pp. 263, 448, 358, 49. Lewes's essay on Austen is reprinted in *Jane Austen: the Critical Heritage*, ed. B. C. Southam (London, 1968); see p. 166 for the passage referred to. An earlier passage (pp. 155–6) contains a comparison of Jane Austen to 'Mr. George Eliot'.

13 George Eliot refers to Jane Austen in her letters as early as 1852. *The George Eliot Letters*, ed. Gordon S. Haight (New Haven, 1954–6) ii, p. 31. She and Lewes read *Emma* aloud early in 1857 (ii, p. 327); *Northanger Abbey* and *Persuasion* were also read at about the same time (ii, p. 319) and a copy of *Sense and Sensibility* was bought and presumably read (ii, p. 326). 'Janet's Repentance' was published serially in the second half of 1857. *Mansfield Park* was read aloud in the summer of 1874 (vi, p. 75); *Persuasion* in the autumn of the same year (vi, p. 76); and *Emma* in the autumn of 1875 (vi, p. 171). *Daniel Deronda* was serialised during 1876.

14 George Eliot, *Scenes of Clerical Life*, ed. David Lodge (Harmondsworth, 1973) p. 18. The Victorian phrase is Julia Kavanagh's, in her *English Women of Letters* (1862); cf. Southam, p. 177.

15 James reviewed George Eliot's novel in the *Nation* in February 1876, and at the end of the same year published 'Daniel Deronda: A Conversation' in the

Atlantic Monthly. Both items are reprinted in Carroll's collection; the second is reproduced as an appendix in *The Great Tradition*. The later phrase occurs in *The Middle Years* (London, 1917) p. 85.

16 The phrase occurs in an unsigned review published in the *Nation* on 9 Nov 1865.

17 *The Complete Tales of Henry James*, ed. Leon Edel (Philadelphia, 1962–1965) I, pp. 333, 300, 139.

18 *The Letters of Henry James*, ed. Percy Lubbock (London, 1920) I, p. 72.

19 Henry James, *Watch and Ward*, with an introduction by Leon Edel (London, 1960) pp. 14–15, 7.

20 *Henry James: the Critical Heritage*, ed. Roger Gard (London, 1968) pp. 50, 66–7, 57.

21 Leon Edel, *Henry James: the Conquest of London 1870–1883* (London, 1962) pp. 395–6.

22 James, *The Portrait of a Lady*, ed. Leon Edel (Boston, 1963) pp. xvii–xviii.

23 Arnold Kettle, *An Introduction to the English Novel* (London, 1953) II, p. 13. Professor Kettle also notes that James's method in *The Portrait of a Lady* is 'precisely the method of *Emma*, except that Jane Austen is rather more scrupulously consistent than Henry James' (p. 15).

24 Reprinted in *Trollope: the Critical Heritage*, ed. Donald Smalley (London, 1969) pp. 509–11.

25 *E. M. Forster: the Critical Heritage*, ed. Philip Gardner (London, 1973) pp. 308, 443; Lionel Trilling, *E. M. Forster* (London, 1944) p. 12.

26 E. M. Forster, *Abinger Harvest* (London, 1936) p. 145.

27 P. N. Furbank and F. J. H. Haskell, 'E. M. Forster', *Paris Review*, I (1953) p. 39.

28 P. N. Furbank, 'The Personality of E. M. Forster', *Encounter* xxxv (Nov 1970) p. 65.

29 Duke Maskell, 'Style and Symbolism in *Howards End*', *Essays in Criticism*, xix (1969) pp. 292–307.

30 Conrad, who receives a full measure of treatment in Leavis's book, seems to me to owe virtually nothing to the Austen-Eliot-James tradition, but a great deal to Dickens: as a matter of biographical fact, we know that, although the English admiration for Jane Austen left him baffled, he had read and re-read Dickens in Polish and in English, and the evidence of such novels as *The Secret Agent* suggests a noteworthy debt to the Dickens of, say, *Bleak House*. Incidentally, Leavis's adjustments to his original text have had the effect, *inter alia*, of rendering his references to the Dickensian element in Conrad less deprecatory.

4 'A Developement of Self': Character and Personality in Jane Austen's Fiction

A. WALTON LITZ

Reviewing a recent work of fantasy and science fiction, Joyce Carol Oates declared that the world of science fiction 'is far more credible than that of Jane Austen.'[1] The comparison is cleverly framed to shock the reader, to challenge his scale of literary values, since of all English and American novelists Jane Austen is perhaps the most secure in her reputation as a writer who delivers a compact and credible fictional world, orderly and sufficient within itself yet tangential at every point to our own disordered lives. In spite of her distance from us in time and experience, and her austere decision to make her fictional world far more limited than her actual observation, most of us are content to live within the created world of Jane Austen's novels. This sense of completeness surely has much to do with the way in which she invents, establishes, and develops the characters in her fiction. I would like to speculate in this essay about Jane Austen's authority in characterisation, and perhaps the best place to begin is with some thoughts about the coherence and apparent inevitability of her created world.

We feel that Jane Austen, like the singing girl in Wallace Stevens' 'The Idea of Order at Key West', stands at the centre of a single reality. We know 'that there never was a world for her/Except the one she sang and, singing, made.' In the works of most other novelists we are asked to shift from one level of reality to another, from one order of truth to another, when we move from character to character or incident to incident: Pip and Wemmick may inhabit the same fictional and physical world, but we judge them by separate standards of reality and probability. The same is true of a modern novel like *Brideshead Revisited*, where – as Waugh acknowledged in his 1959 preface – certain scenes and conversations belong to a different order of reality from that established by the verisimilitude of Charles Ryder's Oxford. 'Julia's outburst about mortal sin and Lord

Marchmain's dying soliloquy' represent a different way of writing from 'the early scenes between Charles and his father', or the Oxford adventures, because the novel deliberately dramatises the distance between two levels of reality.

Nothing like this is conceivable in Jane Austen's fiction. As John Bayley says, in his fine essay on 'The "Irresponsibility" of Jane Austen', Highbury is real 'because there is no alternative to it'.

> Highbury is a real place, as in their different ways Middlemarch and Henry James's Mayfair – even his Boston – are not; and its reality depends on its inescapability. . . . Highbury is known by Jane Austen as Emma knows it by standing at the door of Ford's the draper.[2]

This assertion may beg the question a little, as all our talk about character must, but it is essentially right: 'Of course Jane Austen "made up" Highbury, as all novelists make up their fictions, but it was also the world she lived and had to live in – if it was not we could not live in it as we do and ask the questions about it that we do ask.'[3] When Emma stands for a moment at leisure in the doorway of Ford's the draper, waiting for the scene to compose itself like a picturesque sketch, Jane Austen comments that 'a mind lively and at ease, can do with seeing nothing, and can see nothing that does not answer' (p. 233). This ability to see nothing that is not there, and the nothing that is, marks Jane Austen's achievement in her most self-sufficient novels, *Pride and Prejudice*, *Mansfield Park*, and *Emma*. In part it stems from the apparent stability of the rural society she loved. In his essay on 'Rural Life in England', written around 1817, Washington Irving commented with the sharp awareness of an outsider on this 'settled' quality of rural England. While acknowledging the disturbing effects of recent changes in land distribution, Irving nonetheless found that the villages which Jane Austen took as her subject were solid and miniature worlds, affording 'specimens of the different ranks', and pervaded with a 'moral feeling' that came from the traditional adjustments between individuals and society.

The cohesiveness and stability which are embodied in Jane Austen's major fiction are nowhere more evident than in her technical handling of so-called 'flat' or 'type' characters. Recent critics have tended to speak of these figures as caricatures, but E. M. Forster was more nearly right when he said, in *Aspects of the Novel*, that 'she never stooped to caricature.'

She is a miniaturist, but never two-dimensional. All her characters are round, or capable of rotundity. Even Miss Bates has a mind, even Elizabeth Eliot a heart, and Lady Bertram's moral fervour ceases to vex us when we realize this: the disk has suddenly extended and become a little globe. When the novel is closed, Lady Bertram goes back to the flat, it is true; the dominant impression she leaves can be summed up in a formula. But that is not how Jane Austen conceived her, and the freshness of her reappearances are due to this.[4]

The lifelike characters of comedy may, as Northrop Frye has said, 'owe their consistency to the appropriateness of the stock type which belongs to their dramatic function',[5] but in *Pride and Prejudice* or *Emma* the humorous characters belong to the same order of reality as the heroes and heroines. In his 1843 praise of Jane Austen, Macaulay stressed her ability to present commonplace characters which 'are all as perfectly discriminated from each other as if they were the most eccentric of human beings';[6] and in proof of his claim Macaulay cited the four clergymen – Edward Ferrars, Henry Tilney, Edmund Bertram, Mr Elton – who although they are specimens of a narrow part of the upper middle class are radically different individuals, far removed from the humorous characters of conventional comedy. We might reverse Macaulay's argument (really the obverse truth) and say that the greatest eccentrics in Jane Austen's fiction – even Mr Collins or Miss Bates – have their source of being in the commonplace.

It is this harmony between characters and the base of reality – which is but to say, between characters and action – that made Jane Austen's nineteenth-century critics appeal so often to Shakespeare, and in Aristotelian terms: a critical comparison that may, in the long run, yield more profound insights than the twentieth century's penchant for comparing her art to Henry James's. Walter Scott's remarks on the probability of her characters and incidents, Whately's Aristotelian praise of her ability to 'present us with a clear and *abstracted* view of the general rules themselves' (that is, the neo-classical rules for the imitation of General Nature), Richard Simpson's comment that Jane Austen could not conceive of characters in repose, but only as composite forces unfolded in action: these remind us that some of the most perceptive and enduring assessments of Jane Austen's fiction came out of the tradition of late eighteenth- and nineteenth-century Shakespeare criticism, with its emphasis on psychological essences and the autonomy of dramatic character.[7] The best critics in this tradition, such as Simpson and A. C. Bradley, seem to have a special instinct for Jane Austen's purpose and methods; so it will pay us to put aside for a moment our prejudice against this criticism, and attend to its central theme – that the characters of great art have an apparently independent existence because they are part of a single world, the only world in which we can imagine their existence. Thus Simpson and Bradley can discuss each character in Jane Austen as if they were actors understudying a particular role, and yet never lose sight of some unified design. They are especially good on the minor characters, the *ficelles* and fools, because they appreciate the autonomy of these figures. They can disengage characters from the fiction, discuss them as if they were isolated beings, and then restore them to the dramatic action. Since these Shakespeareans were the exponents of a criticism that was itself a product of the late eighteenth-century readjustment between the universal and the particular, between the world of traditional mimesis and the world evolved from within the mind of the artist, they were unusually well-equipped to explore Jane Austen's transitional methods of characterisation. Although the notion of the 'characteristic' or singular is generally at odds with the neo-classical drive toward unformity, we do not feel this tension in Jane Austen's fiction. We cannot imagine her claiming, as Reynolds does in his *Third Discourse*, that the artist 'corrects' nature, striving toward some central form beyond individual deviations or deformities; but neither can we imagine her joining with Hazlitt in his criticism of Reynolds, where he asserts that 'character is a thing of peculiarity, of striking contrast, of distinction, and not of uniformity.'[8] In her normative art she mediates between these extremes, rejecting the emblematic figures of so much eighteenth-century fiction (especially the Gothic) while stopping short of the merely eccentric or particular. It is a hallmark of her considerable achievement that we can discuss her art in the language of Johnson's *Preface to Shakespeare* or Coleridge's Shakespeare lectures, and feel little strain as we move from one vocabulary to the other.

This is why Simpson, following the lead of Macaulay, could speak of Jane Austen as an artist whose characters 'are all natural, all more or less commonplace, but all discriminated from one another beyond the possibility of confusion, by touches so delicate that they defy analysis, and so true that they elude observation, and only produce the effect by their accumulation.' Jane Austen rejects the isolated portrait, 'in the manner of Theophrastus or La Bruyère', and sees the individual 'not as a solitary being complete in himself, but only as completed in society'.[9] Thus her characters are 'unfolded' in action, are part of a living history, and contain within themselves many potential roles; yet all these potentialities are facets of a radical and unchanging self. Both Jane Austen and her Shakespearean critics would have been baffled by this recent behaviourist definition of the 'personality':

> The learned repertoire of roles is the personality. There is nothing else. There is no 'core' personality underneath the behavior and feelings; there is no 'central' monolithic self which lies beneath the various external manifestations ... The 'self' is a composite of many selves, each of them consisting of a set of self-perceptions, which are specific to one or another major role, specific to the expectations of one or another significant reference group.[10]

In Jane Austen's most assured art, stretching from *Pride and Prejudice* through *Emma*, we encounter an artist who works easily and freely within the widest limits of type and role because she knows that her characters will be ultimately restored to their true selves, living the only lives we can conceive of their living – restored to themselves in those assured last chapters which allow no thought of an alternative world.

There is, of course, ample room for education and improvement in Jane Austen's characters, through example or humiliation or painful self-recognition; but the end result is always some version of a central self. Edmund Bertram finally comes to understand impulses that have always been the best part of his self; Kitty Bennet is much improved through her association with Jane and Elizabeth, and Jane Austen has prepared us for this improvement by giving her a tractable character. Lydia and Mary, on the other hand, have always been themselves, and remain stubbornly the same. When Elizabeth Bennet's follies are revealed to her by Darcy's letter, she cries: 'Till this moment, I never knew myself' (p. 208), as if that self had always been there, waiting to be discovered. And when Emma Woodhouse finally recognises the impropriety and mischievousness of her conduct toward Harriet, Jane Austen calls that painful moment 'a developement of self' (p. 409), using development' not in our modern sense of change and becoming but in the older sense of discovery or disclosure. Emma may learn, with the help of

Knightley, to control or suppress her obsession for playing artist and creating social fictions, but this trait will forever be a part of her 'self'. In Jane Austen's major fiction, we are confronted with a world of Being rather than a world of Becoming.

The final chapters of her novels, therefore, yield the pleasure of a design completed, with no competing possibilities to trouble our minds. The last chapter of *Pride and Prejudice* opens with a note of utter finality:

> Happy for all her maternal feelings was the day on which Mrs. Bennet got rid of her two most deserving daughters. With what delighted pride she afterwards visited Mrs. Bingley and talked of Mrs. Darcy may be guessed. I wish I could say, for the sake of her family, that the accomplishment of her earnest desire in the establishment of so many of her children, produced so happy an effect as to make her a sensible, amiable, well-informed woman for the rest of her life; though perhaps it was lucky for her husband, who might not have relished domestic felicity in so unusual a form, that she still was occasionally nervous and invariably silly. (p. 385)

To confront in the last chapter all the novel's personages, major or minor, intricate or simple, finally acting 'in character', is a large part of our perpetual delight in *Pride and Prejudice* or *Mansfield Park* or *Emma*.

Given this relative stability of ego and environment – the terms of Jane Austen's contract with her reader – characterisation in her major fiction can proceed in a variety of interesting and complementary ways. Jane Austen can describe character directly in the generalised but precise language she inherited from the eighteenth century, the language of Johnson and the essayists; or she can let character reveal itself through drama and dialogue. But running between these extremes are more complicated and indirect strategies of revelation.

One of these involves our double, ironic vision of her central figures, most of whom are amateur artists busy with the work of fiction-making and characterisation. They invent plots, write letters of character analysis, read between the lines of other letters, play games with words and names, discuss absent friends, sketch portraits, collect literary extracts, put on plays, probe motives and arrange matches that have an aesthetic 'rightness' to them. These activities and many more are imitations of the process in which Jane

Austen herself is engaged, and as we follow them with amused delight we gain a fuller sense of the characters as *she* sees them. Elizabeth Bennet, like most of Jane Austen's young ladies, is 'a studier of character' (p. 42), and her distinction between simple and intricate characters can be of great help to us (as Reuben Brower has demonstrated);[11] at the same time, it leads Elizabeth herself into wilful misunderstanding. As a witty and perceptive would-be artist working without a clear understanding of self or society, Elizabeth in the first half of *Pride and Prejudice* constantly but unconsciously reveals her true character as she studies the character of others.

'What think you of books?' said [Darcy], smiling.

'Books – Oh! no. – I am sure we never read the same, or not with the same feelings.'

'I am sorry you think so; but if that be the case, there can at least be no want of subject. – We may compare our different opinions.'

'No – I cannot talk of books in a ball-room; my head is always full of something else.'

'The *present* always occupies you in such scenes – does it?' said he, with a look of doubt.

'Yes, always,' she replied, without knowing what she said, for her thoughts had wandered far from the subject, as soon afterwards appeared by her suddenly exclaiming, 'I remember hearing you once say, Mr. Darcy, that you hardly ever forgave, that your resentment once created was unappeasable. You are very cautious, I suppose, as to its *being created*.'

'I am,' said he, with a firm voice.

'And never allow yourself to be blinded by prejudice?'

'I hope not.'

'It is particularly incumbent on those who never change their opinion, to be secure of judging properly at first.'

'May I ask to what these questions tend?'

'Merely to the illustration of *your* character,' said she, endeavouring to shake off her gravity. 'I am trying to make it out.' (p. 93)

By this point in the novel (the Netherfield ball) we have learned enough of Darcy's pride and Elizabeth's unconscious prejudices to know that the dialogue tends toward an illustration of *her* character, and it is the memory of conversations such as this – 'blind, partial, prejudiced, absurd' – that will later cause Elizabeth such pain and self-knowledge.

In the first half of *Pride and Prejudice* the reader discovers, through the ironies of dramatic action, the central selves of Darcy and Elizabeth. But the action cannot be completed, and the novel 'finished' – in the sense of its world permanently established – until these discoveries made by the reader are shared by the characters themselves. This process entails a difficult but liberating adjustment to reality, such as takes place in the opening scene of Volume Three, where Elizabeth against her will tours the grounds of Pemberley and the great house itself. Walter Scott remarked, in his paraphrase of the plot, that Elizabeth 'does not perceive that she has done a foolish thing until she accidentally visits a very handsome seat and grounds belonging to her admirer',[12] and Scott's much-abused observation is quite true. Many critics have pointed out that Jane Austen's description of the prospect of Pemberley is a covert description of Darcy's character, as well as a material reminder of his wealth and position.

> It was a large, handsome, stone building, standing well on rising ground, and backed by a ridge of high woody hills; – and in front, a stream of some natural importance was swelled into greater, but without any artificial appearance. Its banks were neither formal, nor falsely adorned. Elizabeth was delighted. She had never seen a place for which nature had done more, or where natural beauty had been so little counteracted by an awkward taste. They were all of them warm in their admiration; and at that moment she felt, that to be mistress of Pemberley might be something! (p. 245)

And then, once within the house, we have the prospect as seen by Elizabeth from a window.

> The hill, crowned with wood, from which they had descended, receiving increased abruptness from the distance, was a beautiful object. Every disposition of the ground was good; and she looked on the whole scene, the river, the trees scattered on its banks, and the winding of the valley, as far as she could trace it, with delight. As they passed into other rooms, these objects were taking different positions; but from every window there were beauties to be seen. The rooms were lofty and handsome, and their furniture suitable to the fortune of their proprietor; but Elizabeth saw, with admiration of his taste, that it was neither gaudy nor uselessly fine; with less of splendor, and more real elegance, than the furniture of Rosings. (p. 246)

But it is the enthusiastic praise of the housekeeper, discoursing with a miniature of Darcy before her – 'very like him', we are told – that completes Elizabeth's adjusted view of Darcy's character. Since for Jane Austen character is 'completed in society' – to borrow Richard Simpson's phrase – it is fitting that Elizabeth's revision of Darcy's character involves the material trappings of his social role.

The same psychology is at work when Emma views Donwell Abbey:

> She felt all the honest pride and complacency which her alliance with the present and future proprietor could fairly warrant, as she viewed the respectable size and style of the building, its suitable, becoming, characteristic situation, low and sheltered – its ample gardens stretching down to meadows washed by a stream, of which the Abbey, with all the old neglect of prospect, had scarcely a sight – and its abundance of timber in rows and avenues, which neither fashion nor extravagance had rooted up. – The house was larger than Hartfield, and totally unlike it, covering a good deal of ground, rambling and irregular, with many comfortable and one or two handsome rooms. – It was just what it ought to be, and it looked what it was. (p. 358)

Donwell Abbey, like Knightley, displays no tension between appearance and reality: 'it looked what it was.'

These 'placements' of Darcy and Knightley in a physical environment make one think inevitably of Isabel Archer's uneasy exchange with the more experienced Madame Merle, in Henry James's *The Portrait of a Lady*. They have been discussing a suitor who is only partly hypothetical:

> 'I don't care anything about his house,' said Isabel.
>
> 'That's very crude of you. When you've lived as long as I you'll see that every human being has his shell and that you must take the shell into account. By the shell I mean the whole envelope of circumstances. There's no such thing as an isolated man or woman; we're each of us made up of some cluster of appurtenances. What shall we call our "self"? Where does it begin? where does it end? It overflows into everything that belongs to us – and then it flows back again. I know a large part of myself is in the clothes I choose to wear. I've a great respect for *things*! One's self – for other people – is one's expression of one's self; and one's house, one's furniture, one's garments, the books one reads, the company one keeps – these things are all expressive.'

This was very metaphysical; not more so, however, than several observations Madame Merle had already made. Isabel was fond of metaphysics, but was unable to accompany her friend into this bold analysis of the human personality. 'I don't agree with you. I think just the other way. I don't know whether I succeed in expressing myself, but I know that nothing else expresses me. Nothing that belongs to me is any measure of me; everything's on the contrary a limit, a barrier, and a perfectly arbitrary one. Certainly the clothes which, as you say, I choose to wear, don't express me; and heaven forbid they should!'

'You dress very well,' Madame Merle lightly interposed.

'Possibly; but I don't care to be judged by that. My clothes may express the dressmaker, but they don't express me. To begin with it's not my own choice that I wear them; they're imposed upon me by society.'

'Should you prefer to go without them?' Madame Merle enquired in a tone which virtually terminated the discussion.

(Chapter XIX)

The 'things' at Pemberley and Donwell Abbey are indeed expressive of self, although they speak discreetly: objects in Jane Austen have not yet taken on that troubling and independent existence they have in many later novels. One can easily read the exchange between Isabel and Madame Merle as a dialogue between two halves of Jane Austen's mind or temperament, her allegiance to the free spirit balanced against her recognition of limits and restraints – the two poised most happily in the easy resolutions of *Pride and Prejudice* and *Emma*.

In his fine study of *Character and the Novel*, W. J. Harvey works from a provisional distinction between mimetic and autonomous characters. We say that a mimetic novel is true, probable, 'real' if it embodies the forms of general nature, or points to the contours of a known society – Regency England, for example. We say that a novel of autonomous characters is true, probable, 'real' if it hangs together internally, if its characters are full and complete participants in the verbal structure: to paraphrase I. A. Richards, we substitute truth of coherence for truth of reference. These are treacherous distinctions, as Harvey well knows, always subject to qualification and adjustment, but the historical drift in fiction from mimetic to autonomous notions of character is indisputable. A moderate statement of the contemporary critical position would be

that of Martin Price, in his essay 'The Other Self', where Price
contends that 'the character we admire as the result of loving
attention is something constructed by conventions as arbitrary as any
other' and urges a criticism attentive to the artifice of characterisation.[13] More extreme would be the recent formalist-structuralist
theories, where even autonomy of character is frequently called into
doubt, and where the model is those modern works of fiction that
resist identity and dramatise a 'seepage' between persons and
environment. Jonathan Culler has summed up this view in his survey
of *Structuralist Poetics*:

> ... the general ethos of structuralism runs counter to the notions
> of individuality and rich psychological coherence which are often
> applied to the novel. Stress on the interpersonal and conventional
> systems which traverse the individual, which make him a space
> in which forces and events meet rather than an individuated
> essence, leads to a rejection of a prevalent conception of character
> in the novel: that the most successful and 'living' characters are
> richly delineated autonomous wholes, clearly distinguished from
> others by physical and psychological characteristics. This notion
> of character, structuralists would say, is a myth.
> ... [This] argument is often conflated with a historical distinction.
> If, as Foucault says, man is simply a fold in our knowledge who
> will disappear in his present form as soon as the configuration of
> knowledge changes, it is scarcely surprising that a movement
> which claims to have participated in this change should view the
> notion of the rich and autonomous character as the recuperative
> strategy of another age. ... The expectations and procedures of
> assimilation appropriate to nineteenth-century novels with their
> individuated psychological essences fail before the faceless protago-
> nists of modern fiction or the picaresque heroes of earlier novels.[14]

However, if we leave aside this modern assault upon the very
notions of identity and the 'self', I think we can say that Jane Austen
at her best managed to create characters which satisfy the broadest
range of critical expectations: they are both mimetic and autonomous, matching our sense of external reality and our sense of
structural completeness. Jane Austen is totally aware of the artifice
in her rendering of character (her heroines reveal this in their games
of character-building), but she would not have understood the
following modish statement of a 'universally acknowledged' critical
truth.

The distinction between characters and actual persons is an absolute one. Characters are no more like persons than, to use Degas' summation of a similar distinction in art, the air of the old masters is like the air we breathe. Everyone knows this, of course ... characters are schematic (as no person, however dull, is).[15]

Jane Austen could conceive of characters as both schematic and 'like' actual persons, and this achievement has to do with her single world, its stability of self and manners; it also has to do with the way in which the characters themselves, within the created circle of the novel, have a tendency to behave as secret artists and 'studiers of character'. A combination of absolute naturalness and absolute self-consciousness has been the foundation of Jane Austen's enduring reputation, gaining her equal praise – and equally illuminating criticism – from nineteenth-century Shakespeareans and modern formalists.

So far this essay has concentrated on the works of Jane Austen's middle period, especially *Pride and Prejudice* and *Emma*. *Northanger Abbey* and *Sense and Sensibility* have been neglected because, in spite of their later revisions, they still display some of the schematic qualities of late eighteenth-century fiction which Jane Austen ultimately overcame; but *Persuasion* has been pushed to one side for a different reason. In company with the Last Work, *Sanditon*, *Persuasion* reflects a more unsettled artistic vision, and embodies a somewhat different view of the self. To return to Madame Merle and Isabel Archer: tempting as it is to convert their exchange into a dialogue within Jane Austen's fictive imagination, a certain amount of trimming is required. What has intervened between Emma's 'developement of self' and Madame Merle's question, 'What shall we call our "self"?', is that acceptance of dynamic growth and unpredictable change which marks the nineteenth-century novel: a discovery of self has given way to a 'development' of self in our modern sense of the term, involved with doubt and indeterminacy. Of course, these tendencies had always been latent in Jane Austen's art, but they were suppressed or adroitly handled, just as the social and economic changes of her time were suppressed or controlled in the novels before *Persuasion*. The Gardiners, for example, may be representatives of a new and unsettling social energy, but they are easily processed into the comic ending of *Pride and Prejudice*, and become part of Pemberley: the stable self remains the centre of a stable world. But in *Persuasion* we feel the pressure of an uncertain and even hostile social climate, and the disturbing possibility of alterations in the self. Just the fact that the time of the novel is 'the present' (1814–15), while the other novels are somewhat distanced from the contemporary in opinions and manners, shows Jane Austen's new preoccupation with uncertainty and change. This may be seen in the more intrusive pressures of the material environment, of physical constrictions and discomforts, and the repeated comparisons of the self with the natural world in all its mutability.

More evidence of a new perspective in *Persuasion* may be found in the novel's beginnings and endings. Sir Walter's introduction through the pages of the *Baronetage* (a fiction within a fiction) is a harsh reminder of what Madame Merle's expressive circumstances can become if they swallow up the self. Jane Austen's flat statement that 'Vanity was the beginning and the end of Sir Walter Elliot's character' (p. 4) can hardly be imagined in the earlier novels. In sharp contrast, Anne is 'only Anne', aware of her own potential nothingness; although her subjective grasp of self is firmer than that of any other Austen heroine, Anne knows that alterations in time and place may threaten the self. The entire first chapter of *Persuasion* is permeated with a sense of time passing and irretrievably lost, of youth and 'bloom' never to be regained. The thirteen years that have passed since Lady Elliot's death become a litany ('Thirteen winters' revolving frosts . . . thirteen springs shewn their blossoms'), and it is tempting to connect these years with the thirteen years of inexorable change mentioned by Jane Austen in her 'Advertisement' to *Northanger Abbey*.

> This little work was finished in the year 1803, and intended for immediate publication. . . . some observation is necessary upon those parts of the work which thirteen years have made comparatively obsolete. The public are entreated to bear in mind that thirteen years have passed since it was finished, many more since it was begun, and that during that period, places, manners, books, and opinions have undergone considerable change.

Similarly, the last chapter of *Persuasion* does not leave us with the composed sense of 'it is finished', of a world achieved. Anne must still pay 'the tax of quick alarm' (p. 252), which encompasses not just 'the dread of a future war' but the uneasy intuition of life's random disasters. In sharp contrast with Jane Austen's other novels, we are left with no stable place or home in which we can imagine Anne's future happiness.

Although D. H. Lawrence had other aims in mind when he said, in 'A Propos of *Lady Chatterley's Lover*', that Jane Austen 'typifies "personality" instead of character, the sharp knowing in apartness instead of knowing in togetherness',[16] we can easily use his terms to define the difference between *Persuasion* and the earlier fictions. 'Personality' in our modern psychological meaning of the word was a late, eighteenth-century arrival: before that time the term referred to the physical person, the quality of being human. Some of this older meaning lingers on in Jane Austen's usage of the word 'person', but certainly her perception of the self in *Persuasion* – with its emphasis on estrangement and isolation – demands our modern sense of the term. To borrow the sociological language of Durkheim and his followers, the life of a stable ego *solidaire* with society threatens, in *Persuasion*, to give way to a condition of *anomie*, of unplanned and mysterious growth.

Leaving aside possible historical reasons for Jane Austen's changing view of the self, and concentrating on her personal vision, it seems clear that *Persuasion* – in spite of its 'comic' ending – shades constantly toward the tragic. As Mary McCarthy once observed, traditional characterisation is 'seldom accomplished outside of comedy or without the fixative of comedy', since the comic element is the permanent strain in all of us, and thus an ally of the unchanging self.[17] Jane Austen's heroes and heroines before *Persuasion* may enlarge or improve themselves through self-education, but they remain stable, and it is the comic element in them or around them (especially the 'flat' characters) that helps to fix our notion of their 'selves'. One sign of the new departure in *Persuasion* is the thinning out or dulling of the comic types, those we know will never change.

And even in *Sanditon*, where Jane Austen returned with gusto to the comic effects of her earliest fiction (probably as a defence against illness and despair), we feel that the world of *Pride and Prejudice* or *Emma* is gone forever. The eccentrics and grotesques in *Sanditon* are there for a different – and darker – purpose. The opening of the fragment, the 'improvement' episodes, and especially the closing scene – all speak of accidents, alterations, uncertainties of perspective. Charlotte's final glimpse of Clara Brereton in the mist as 'something White & Womanish' (p. 426) is an emblem of Jane Austen's new openness. With the other major unfinished work, *The*

Watsons (c. 1803), we have little difficulty in imagining satisfactory endings, but *Sanditon* is an enigma. As Mary Lascelles says, none of the earlier novels 'would, if broken off short at the eleventh chapter, have left us in such uncertainty as to the way in which it was going to develop'.[18] But regardless of how the Last Work might have ended, or the direction that Jane Austen's art might have taken, we can be sure that she would never have turned back from a world of Becoming to a world where characters can simply Be.

NOTES

1 Joyce Carol Oates, review of *Guernica Night* by Barry N. Malzberg, *New York Times Book Review*, 21 Sep 1975, p. 18.

2 John Bayley, 'The "Irresponsibility" of Jane Austen', in *Critical Essays on Jane Austen*, ed. B. C. Southam (London, 1968) p. 9.

3 Ibid.

4 E. M. Forster, *Aspects of the Novel* (New York, 1927) pp. 113–14.

5 Northrop Frye, *Anatomy of Criticism* (Princeton, 1957) p. 172.

6 *Edinburgh Review*, Jan. 1843. Reprinted in *Jane Austen: the Critical Heritage*, ed. B. C. Southam (London, 1968) p. 122.

7 See *The Critical Heritage*, especially pp. 59–61, 93, 249–50.

8 William Hazlitt, 'On Certain Inconsistencies in Sir Joshua Reynolds's Discourses', in *Table-Talk*, World's Classics (London, 1901) p. 185. For background to this debate see Houghton W. Taylor, ' "Particular Character": An Early Phase of a Literary Evolution', *PMLA*, 60 (Mar 1945) pp. 161–74.

9 *The Critical Heritage*, p. 249 (1870 review of the *Memoir*).

10 Orville E. Brim, Jr., 'Personality Development as Role-Learning' (1960) quoted in Martin Price. 'The Other Self: Thoughts about Character in the Novel', in *Imagined Worlds: Essays on some English Novels and Novelists in Honour of John Butt*, ed. Maynard Mack and Ian Gregor (London, 1968) p. 282.

11 Reuben A. Brower, 'Light and Bright and Sparkling: Irony and Fiction in *Pride and Prejudice*', in *The Fields of Light* (New York, 1951) pp. 164–81.

12 *The Critical Heritage*, p. 65.

13 Martin Price, 'The Other Self', p. 293.

14 Jonathan Culler, *Structuralist Poetics* (Ithaca, N.Y., 1975) pp. 230–1.

15 Rawdon Wilson, 'On Character: A Reply to Martin Price', *Critical Inquiry*, 2 (autumn 1975) p. 194. In this response to an essay by Martin Price on Forster's *A Passage to India*, Price's view is developed with a rigour and inflexibility that Price himself would never accept.

16 D. H. Lawrence, 'A Propos of *Lady Chatterley's Lover*', in *Sex, Literature and Censorship*, ed. Harry T. Moore (New York, 1953) p. 119. First published in 1930.

17 Mary McCarthy, 'Characters in Fiction', in *On the Contrary* (New York, 1961) p. 288.

18 Mary Lascelles, *Jane Austen and her Art* (Oxford, 1939) p. 39. The fragment actually contains twelve chapters.

5 Properties and Possessions in Jane Austen's Novels [1]

BARBARA HARDY

Ever since Fielding designed an appropriate dwelling for Mr All-worthy in *Tom Jones*, the houses in fiction have been carefully planned and furnished. Allworthy's house is the best of Gothic, and can rival the Grecian style. Its situation is sufficiently low to be sheltered from the north-east by an oak grove, sufficiently elevated to yield fine prospects. Its lawns and tree-clumps are landscaped by man; its cascades, lake and meandering river by nature. The rooms in the front enjoy views of the park, waters, ruined abbey, villages, animals and a cloud-topped ridge of high mountains. Its river reaches a sea, its mountains are lost in sky. Extensive without, it is commodious within. House and environs possess unity and variety, look out on civilisation and nature, are products of both but owe more to nature than to art. The view was drawn, with a fine balance of sobriety and wit, from Glastonbury Tor, near Fielding's birth-place, and the house probably draws on features of Ralph Allen's house at Prior Park, near Bath, and Sharpham Park, near Glaston-bury, combined and varied by the novelist's natural powers and artifice.

Jane Austen must have remembered these eloquent advantages when accommodating Darcy at Pemberley, and Fielding's principles of ironic symbolism may also have determined the choice of North-anger Abbey for General Tilney, Rosings for Lady Catherine de Bourgh, Mansfield Park for the Bertrams and Sotherton for Mrs Rushworth. Fielding's comic irony held Allworthy's great house and prospects at arm's length from the reader's judgement, dangerously grand, suspiciously eloquent, an ideal environment for an ideal or idealising human occupant. Jane Austen's comic imagination foun-ded her sympathetic habitats more firmly, more craftily, and yet more naturally in her fictions, by using her characters as architects and builders. It is their insight and projection which make the houses so sympathetic. The pathetic fallacy is extended and civilised. Her symbolic houses are conspicuous instances in an art inclined always to merge symbol in surface, but their symbolism is an aspect of her characters. It may well have been her assimilations and variations of Fielding which consolidated the symbolic environment as a tradition in the novel. Fielding's design is passed on through Jane Austen to the architects of Thrushcross Grange, Wuthering Heights, Gateshead, Thornfield Manor, Ferndean, Lowood, the House of Usher, Lowick, Gardencourt, Poynton and Castle de Stancy. Throughout the nineteenth century houses grew more like their owners, in style and contents.

Jane Austen placed the sympathetic habitat within the minds of her characters but its existence is not wholly subjective. She invented the suitably malleable material which made the house the right kind of shell for its occupant. She saw environment as a case both forming and formed by people. Her houses are animated, or fail to be animated, by the life led within their walls and beneath their roofs. They are restored, improved, or left unimproved, by likely people. Households, as well as owners, partake of this life of houses. The houses accommodate guests as well as hosts. Homes are significantly commodious or restricted, old or modern, elegant or heavy, big or small. They are good shelters, hives with isolated cells, prisons or protections. They stifle or facilitate life, welcome or fail to welcome the visitor. Roofs and walls allow for growth or enclose life. Houses are beautiful or ugly, but their beauty is more than skin-deep. In Jane Austen gardens are the woods where destinies are found and lost, in small evergreen shrubberies, ordered wildernesses, by dangerous ha-has and gates, in damp grounds and old temples, by rich lawns and fertile waters.

Houses and grounds begin to be fully animated in *Northanger Abbey*. It may have been the demands of a plot requiring a Gothic abbey with an unGothic atmosphere which developed Jane Austen's imaginative architecture. We see Northanger through Catherine Morland's eyes and imagination. At first sight Northanger is a disappointment to her, her 'passion for ruins', second only to her 'passion for Henry Tilney', having formed great expectations from Mrs Radcliffe's castles in Italy. (She has already been disappointed by not going to Blaize Castle.) Her first impressions are obscure:

As they drew near the end of their journey, her impatience for a sight of the abbey – for some time suspended by his conversation

on subjects very different – returned in full force, and every bend
in the road was expected with solemn awe to afford a glimpse of
its massy walls of grey stone, rising amidst a grove of ancient
oaks, with the last beams of the sun playing in beautiful splendour
on its high Gothic windows. But so low did the building stand,
that she found herself passing through the great gates of the lodge
into the very grounds of Northanger, without having discerned
even an antique chimney.

She knew not that she had any right to be surprized, but there
was a something in this mode of approach which she certainly
had not expected. To pass between lodges of a modern appearance, to find herself with such ease in the very precincts of the
abbey, and driven so rapidly along a smooth, level road of fine
gravel, without obstacle, alarm or solemnity of any kind, struck
her as odd and inconsistent. (*NA*, p. 161)

When she finds herself inside, the furniture is too modern, the
light too bright, the walls too clean, even the authentic windows
disturbingly clear. She later finds the restorations too effective, and
the servants' quarters too convenient. As an abbey it is lacking in
mystery, insufficiently sinister. But Catherine's passion works hard
on its possibilities, aided by her real insight, which has already
detected something wrong in her host and his family's life. Northanger turns out after all to be the right kind of dwelling for Jane
Austen's version of Montoni, whose modern tyrannies are every bit
as bad and potent as those imagined by Mrs Radcliffe in *The
Mysteries of Udolpho*, and who does bring 'misery' to the heroine.
Host and guest are set at cross-purposes in a place designed to
mislead them both. What General Tilney offers is as obscure to his
guest as her expectations – in all senses – are unknown to him. He
is the owner of the Abbey, his autocracy ordering his household,
demanding its prompt attendance in the elegant dining-room on the
stroke of five, keeping a good table, ingratiatingly belittling his
possessions but demanding admiration for contrivance and property,
and evicting his guest the minute he discovers her unsuitability for
his purposes. Hospitality can be no more effectively and thoroughly
breached, even in the Gothic novels where the heroines were lodged
in a solitary and gloomy room. The ironic symbolism of Jane Austen's
house is a comic but bitter account of a family and its life, a host
and his predatory entertainments.

The symbolism of the house depends on its contents as well as its structure. Northanger Abbey first provides objects for Catherine's literary imagination to embellish. Houses are shells, but not empty shells, and Jane Austen provides an inner coating of things which joins people with building. She goes beyond Fielding to create a house filled with expressive objects. The things in Northanger Abbey are set in action as dramatic properties, but are so thoroughly imagined in relation to the people who own and use them that they invoke a variety of human responses, answering to human imagination, needs, appetites and wishes. Almost everything in the Abbey carries the imprint of the improving hand, but Jane Austen's solid sense of likelihood prevents her from making merely melodramatic furniture and fittings. The improving hand isn't only the grasping hand of General Tilney, but the neutrally recorded hand of his father. Some part is played by the sensible housekeeping of Eleanor, who decided to keep the old chest in Catherine's room as a useful container for 'hats and bonnets'. But General Tilney's guardianship and responsibility are emphasised. He shows Catherine the disappointing rooms and their contents. Having hoped 'for the smallest divisions, and the heaviest stone-work, for painted glass, dirt and cobwebs', she finds the unstained window-panes, despite their arches, too large. Her self-deprecating host thinks she is looking for more opulence, not more antiquity, and his promise of fine gilding elsewhere is interrupted only by his passion for punctuality at meals. As Catherine gets ready for dinner in her room, she is disappointed by the papered walls, anticipating the future fictional occasion when her fastidious descendant, Henry James's Mrs Gereth, is kept awake by the wallpaper of Waterbath, having been accustomed to the walls of Poynton, unsullied by any scrap of pasted paper.

Jane Austen dramatises her heroine's attentiveness to the first object that catches her attention, the 'immense heavy chest' which looks so antique:

> She advanced and examined it closely: it was of cedar, curiously inlaid with some darker wood, and raised, about a foot from the ground, on a carved stand of the same. The lock was silver, though tarnished from age; at each end were the imperfect remains of handles also of silver, broken perhaps prematurely by some strange violence; and, on the centre of the lid, was a mysterious cypher, in the same metal. Catherine bent over it intently, but without being able to distinguish any thing with certainty. She could not, in whatever direction she took it, believe the last letter

to be a *T*; and yet that it should be anything else in that house was a circumstance to raise no common degree of astonishment. If not originally their's, by what strange events could it have fallen into the Tilney family? (*NA*, pp. 163–4)

This is the first of Catherine's necessary object-lessons. The heavy old chest is eloquent of ordinary life and ordinary likelihood: it opens, after her strenuous efforts, to reveal the most innocent linen, 'a white cotton counterpane, properly folded, reposing at one end of the chest in undisputed possession'. The object seems to flout her by its very blandness. In creating this sly suggestiveness, Jane Austen draws on a mild comic animism which is found less often in the novels than in her letters, where the play of comic imagination is free to make the nonsensical jokes that intimacy will tolerate and even enjoy: 'The Tables are come, & give general contentment. . . . – They are both covered with green baize & send their best Love' (*Letters*, p. 82).

In *Northanger Abbey* Jane Austen seems to remember Don Quixote, archetypal mis-imaginer. She makes Catherine follow up 'the adventure of the chest' with the second adventure of the 'high, old-fashioned black cabinet'. It impresses her as having been strangely lying in wait, unobserved in its alcove during her first inspection of the room. It also seems mysteriously reminiscent of the ebony cabinet in Henry Tilney's Gothic parody. It does not fit the object in Henry's tale exactly, as Catherine's candour has to admit: 'It was not absolutely ebony and gold; but it was Japan, black and yellow Japan of the handsomest kind; and as she held her candle, the yellow had very much the effect of gold.' She is observant, as well as honest, and this object is also described minutely, as she examines it minutely. So also are the all-too-clearly discriminated contents of its drawers, discovered with chagrin in the light of day to be bills listing 'Shirts, stockings, cravats and waistcoats', items of expenditure on 'letters, hair-powder, shoe-string and breeches-ball', together with the larger paper enclosing the rest, the farrier's bill for poulticing a chestnut mare. The inventory of everyday life joins with the natural contents of the chest to chasten the heroine's imagination. Catherine feels rebuked as a corner of the chest 'catches her eye', in another mildly animistic stroke of comic play. But a third trial by objects awaits her in the furniture of the deceased mother's room. Instead of the Radcliffean objects of her book-lined imagination (like the black veil which has arrested her

earlier in the novel) what shocks her is a large well-dusted room
with 'a bright Bath stove, mahogany wardrobes and neatly-painted
chairs, on which the warm beams of a western sun gaily poured
through two sash windows'.

The irony makes a neat reversal, for the objects are indeed startling. Most of the things in the Abbey are sinister too in their modern
fashion. The decaying part of the quadrangle has been pulled down
to make room for new offices without any thought of 'uniformity
of architecture'. The subdued emblem of restoration looks ahead
to George Eliot's *Daniel Deronda* and to Thomas Hardy's symbolism
of aesthetic unity in *A Laodicean*, his Victorian version of *Northanger Abbey*, complete with sympathetic habitat and romantic
heroine. 'The General's improving hand' has made some of those
changes which cause Catherine 'almost' to 'rave'. The objects in his
house are the instruments of display and solicitation. He offers the
breakfast set:

> He was enchanted by her approbation of his taste, confessed it to
> be neat and simple, thought it right to encourage the manufacture
> of his country; and for his part, to his uncritical palate, the tea
> was as well flavoured from the clay of Staffordshire, as from that
> of Dresden or Sêve. But this was quite an old set, purchased two
> years ago. (*NA*, p. 175)

Every single word of the General's humble and pastoral apology
is false. In his own house, and in Henry's interestingly incomplete
Parsonage, he uses things and places to flatter himself and the
hoped-for heiress. If the heroine is wrong about her host, he is
equally wrong about his guest. Neither of them is, however, completely mistaken. He is a villain, and she is the heroine. If he is
proffering and praising things for the purpose of his imaginative
desires, so is she. And she is not entirely wrong about the objects in
the story. The portrait of Mrs Tilney which hangs significantly in
Eleanor's room, and not in the drawing-room, is scarcely conspicuous
on its first appearance, but that 'mild and pensive countenance' is
highly expressive in retrospect. It is unlike the mysterious painting in
Henry's parody, but its echo is not simply dissonant. The twists and
turns of burlesque and bathos, parody and surprise, are perfectly
matched in the complex behaviour of the objects.

It seems significant that the single object in the Abbey which is
in no way associated with General Tilney is a hyacinth, the only sign
of spring and natural growth at Northanger Abbey. One of those

small indexes of the advancing year which Jane Austen places so
discreetly into the action, it is mentioned briefly but is not visually
present. The hyacinth is part of Catherine's aesthetic advance in
appreciation, and is associated with Eleanor Tilney's nature. It is
brought into the breakfast conversation by Catherine's desire to
change the subject:

> 'What beautiful hyacinths! – I have just learnt to love a hyacinth.'
>   'And how might you learn? – By accident or argument?'
>   'Your sister taught me; I cannot tell how. Mrs. Allen used to
> take pains, year after year, to make me like them; but I never
> could, till I saw them the other day in Milsom-street; I am
> naturally indifferent about flowers.'
>   'But now you love a hyacinth. So much the better. You have
> gained a new source of enjoyment, and it is well to have as many
> holds upon happiness as possible. Besides, a taste for flowers is
> always desirable in your sex, as a means of getting you out of
> doors, and tempting you to more frequent exercise than you would
> otherwise take. And though the love of a hyacinth may be rather
> domestic, who can tell, the sentiment once raised, but you may
> in time come to love a rose?' (*NA*, p. 174)

The object is embedded in the natural flow of talk. So also is the
other innocent object in Catherine's adventures with things, the fine
netting cotton to be matched by Isabella which she hopes to hear of
in her friend's letter, only to be disappointed by a grimmer tale of
prices and values.

Northanger Abbey was a splendid environment for Jane Austen's
object-making imagination. In *Sense and Sensibility* she continues to
play with the device of appropriate things in appropriate places,
always locating description in the mind of her characters. Places and
objects are animated as they become prominent to people, and are
proportioned by individual viewpoint. The novel begins with Norland, so it is never described; its objects are invoked only as they
become subjects of conversation, as objects of individual response.
In the second chapter, the abstract nature of John and Fanny Dashwood's mean acquisitiveness is made plain through their duet about
money. There is a penultimate diminution as we move from the
smallest sum to 'some little present of furniture' which is made even
less by being unspecified. Even this is transformed into a minus
quantity, as Fanny reminds John that Mrs Dashwood will be taking
off 'all the china, plate, and linen' of Stanhill, her former home:

'Her house will therefore be almost completely fitted up as soon as she takes it.'

'That is a material consideration undoubtedly. A valuable legacy indeed! And yet some of the plate would have been a very pleasant addition to our own stock here.'

'Yes; and the set of breakfast china is twice as handsome, . . . in my opinion, for any place *they* can ever afford to live in.' (*S&S*, p. 13)

Jane Austen's wit is never quieter in its damage than in the line 'That is a material consideration undoubtedly'. The theme of material considerations permeates the society of the novel. It is an environment in which sense and sensibility are formed, tested, falsified, or improved.

In Marianne's enthusiastic nostalgia, Norland is curiously unspecific, invoked through its 'dead leaves', and is as vague in her raptures as in Elinor's refusal to be moved by them. Compared with the colours and motions of Shelley's autumnal rapture, the leaves are imprecisely felt, small indexes of Marianne's unobservant and stereotyped feeling for nature:

'Oh!' cried Marianne, 'with what transporting sensations have I formerly seen them fall! How have I delighted, as I walked, to see them driven in showers about me by the wind! What feelings have they, the season, the air altogether inspired! Now there is no one to regard them. They are seen only as a nuisance, swept hastily off, and driven as much as possible from the sight.'

'It is not every one,' said Elinor, 'who has your passion for dead leaves.' (*S&S*, pp. 87–8)

Marianne's response to nature lacks both the precision and the openness of the more rational romanticism of Fanny Price and Anne Elliot. But vague though it is, Marianne's sensibility rebukes the insensibilities of John and Fanny Dashwood. When John boasts about the plans for Fanny's new greenhouse and flower-garden which are to replace the 'old thorns' and 'old walnut trees', Elinor prudently decides not to tell her sister. The relative lack of possessiveness and materialism in Mrs Dashwood and her daughters is shown in the impetuous choice of Barton Cottage. They decide to move before they have seen their new home, sending their possessions round by sea – another small detail which deprives John Dashwood of any opportunity to help, and shows Jane Austen's thoroughness of imagination. No object is too small for the author's providential care as author. When the family arrives in Barton, there is a minutely detailed description, from which one could draw a plan.

The environment is important as it is received by the individual experience. The smallness of the house invokes various responses: Mrs Dashwood's unpractical plans for improvement, Elinor's controlled rejection of the need for a new grate in the spare bedchamber, Mr Palmer's rude criticism of the low-pitched roof and Willoughby's speech about the cottage which protests a romantic disregard of great possessions, and is typical of him in its glib and superficial reaction. He means what he says, but his sensibility is quite as unreliable as insincerity:

'You would rob it of its simplicity by imaginary improvement! and this dear parlour, in which our acquaintance first began, and in which so many happy hours have been since spent by us together, you would degrade to the condition of a common entrance, and every body would be eager to pass through the room which has hitherto contained within itself, more real accommodation and comfort than any other apartment of the handsomest dimensions in the world could possibly afford.' (*S&S*, pp. 73–4)

Even Robert Ferrars, the essential fool of the novel, makes his contribution:

'For my own part,' said he, 'I am excessively fond of a cottage; there is always so much comfort, so much elegance about them. . . .

'Some people imagine that there can be no accommodations, no space in a cottage; but this is all a mistake. I was last month at my friend Elliott's near Dartford. Lady Elliott wished to give a dance. "But how can it be done?" said she; "my dear Ferrars, do tell me how it is to be managed. There is not a room in this cottage that will hold ten couple, and where can the supper be?" *I* immediately saw that there could be no difficulty in it, so I said, "My dear Lady Elliott, do not be uneasy. The dining parlour will admit eighteen couple with ease; card-tables may be placed in the drawing-room; the library may be open for tea and other refreshments; and let the supper be set out in the saloon." Lady Elliott was delighted with the thought. We measured the dining-room, and found it would hold exactly eighteen couple, and the affair was arranged precisely after my plan. So that, in fact, you see, if people do but know how to set about it, every comfort may be as well enjoyed in a cottage as in the most spacious dwelling.' (S&S, pp. 251–2)

The variants of materialism are largely demonstrated through things of price and value. Marianne's protested disregard of wealth is tested by Elinor's quotation of real prices and incomes, as she compares her smaller 'wealth' with Marianne's larger 'competence'. There is a crucial side-scene in the jeweller's shop, Gray's, in Sackville Street. As we are carefully told, Elinor is there to negotiate 'the exchange of a few old-fashioned jewels of her mother' and John Dashwood 'to bespeak Fanny a seal'. Robert Ferrars flourishes his self-regarding and trivial materialism in his nonsensical dallyings with toothpick-cases, chronicled by Jane Austen in appropriate pomp and circumstance:

> At last the affair was decided. The ivory, the gold, and the pearls, all received their appointment, and the gentleman having named the last day on which his existence could be continued without the possession of the toothpick-case, drew on his gloves with leisurely care . . . (S&S, p. 221)

Miss Steele's attentiveness to objects is silly, but she is more concerned than Robert Ferrars with the world outside. Her trivial-mindedness is curious, and takes stock of Marianne's price and value. 'Minute observation and minute curiosity' are chronicled through their inventory of dress, number of gowns, cost of washing, annual allowance, value and make of gown, 'the colour of her shoes, and the arrangement of her hair'. Jane Austen does not just present and criticise sartorial passion, as George Eliot is inclined to do in *Middlemarch*, where to care about clothes is nearly always immoral. Jane Austen is more tolerant and more precise. She discriminates between feelings for dress. Miss Steele joins her crude commercial interest in the price-tags to the smart stylishness of Willoughby's choice, Miss Grey, the elegant propriety of Lady Middleton, and the dandyism of Robert Ferrars. In *Northanger Abbey* the undemanding but total sartorial energies of Mrs Allen are balanced against the acceptable and natural vanities of Catherine Morland, and the flaunting of Isabella Thorpe, who shares a taste for coquelicot ribbons with her author. In *Mansfield Park*, the complacent self-regard of Lady Bertram is roused to lend her maid to Fanny, though characteristically too late. Fanny's own doubtful pleasure in the gown Sir Thomas gives her for Maria's wedding, worn for that first dinner at the Parsonage and admired by Edmund with a precise eye for its 'glossy spot' because Miss Crawford has one 'something the same' (*MP*, p. 222), is beautifully placed.

Jane Austen's letters to Cassandra show a constant but constantly self-amused preoccupation with dress, and this aspect of the human concern with things is dramatically varied and frequently tolerated. We are made to feel that Jane Austen knows everything about her characters. It is more than frivolous when she says she always suspected that Mrs Darcy's favourite colour was yellow, Mrs Bingley's green (*Letters*, p. 310).

Her knowledge of her characters' attitudes to houses, clothes and accessories extends to other creature comforts. Mrs Jennings's harmless indulgences of the flesh show the largeness of her nature. She is facile, generous, kind, compassionate and likes to enjoy life. She presses old Constantia wine and dried cherries on Marianne's disappointed heart, to be astonished when they don't work. She is eager to help other people to the pleasures of the world and her 'ample jointure' is described in the perfect adjective. She describes to Elinor the joys of Colonel Brandon's place in the country with appropriate gusto:

> 'Delaford is a nice place, I can tell you; exactly what I call a nice old fashioned place, full of comforts and conveniences; quite shut in with great garden walls that are covered with the best fruit-trees in the country: and such a mulberry tree in one corner! Lord! how Charlotte and I did stuff the only time we were there! Then, there is a dove-cote, some delightful stewponds, and a very pretty canal; and every thing, in short, that one could wish for: and, moreover, it is close to the church, and only a quarter of a mile from the turnpike-road, so 'tis never dull, for if you only go and sit up in an old yew arbour behind the house, you may see all the carriages that pass along. Oh! 'tis a nice place! A butcher hard by in the village, and the parsonage-house within a stone's throw. To my fancy, a thousand times prettier than Barton Park, where they are forced to send three miles for their meat, and have not a neighbour nearer than your mother.' (*S&S*, pp. 196–7)

Unlike the Dashwoods and the Steele sisters, Mrs Jennings is a materialist with nothing mean about her – she is a Wife of Bath whose pleasures are of the table rather than the bed, though Jane

Austen may mean more than she finds it decorous to say. Her language is crammed with appreciations, her very proverbs appetitive: 'One shoulder of mutton, you know, drives another down.' The phrase may be on the gross side, but her author comes to a not dissimilar, if more elegantly expressed, conclusion. There is no doubt about Jane Austen's sense of her quality as well as her limitations. She is a tolerant character, and her fleshliness is thoroughly understood and tolerated by her author.

When Margaret Dashwood puts in a bid for memorability by imagining that they have all been left a fortune apiece, everyone, as Edward Ferrars says, chooses appropriate objects. It is the individuality of her people's needs and the desires which shapes Jane Austen's object-world. Like the elaborately detailed fiction of Thackeray, Henry James, Arnold Bennett and Scott Fitzgerald, her novels establish a sense of social surfaces and manners. We can date and describe clothes, houses, furniture, food, drink and means of transport through the information in the novels. But in the novels of Thackeray, James, Bennett and Scott Fitzgerald information is dispersed through generalised and complete descriptions. Whenever there is a room, or a person, we see its furniture and its clothing. This does not mean that there is no discrimination or that objects and places are not dramatically expressive. The kitchen and the factory in Bennett's *Anna of the Five Towns* play an essential role in the affective life of the characters, and Gatsby's shirts are part of his style and his imagination. But all the rooms and clothes in these novels are solidly specified. Mrs Lowder's plutocratically hideous drawing-room in *The Wings of the Dove* and Maggie's dress in *The Golden Bowl* are eloquent of their possessors in many ways, but James is visibly the describing source. The food, drink, furniture, ornaments and service in *Vanity Fair*, *The Newcomes* and *The Virginians* tell us a great deal about class, income, households, characters and countries, but it is Thackeray who sets and specifies the scene. Jane Austen keeps very strictly to what appears to be her self-created rule of characteristic description. If someone in the novel is not registering the appearance, cost or savour of things, they are kept out. There is enough variety of materialism in all the novels to give a full social range, but it is not her habit to describe every house, every meal, everyone's clothes, all the furniture. Objects come in as they strike the characters, sometimes vaguely, sometimes clearly, sometimes lovingly, sometimes obsessionally, sometimes stupidly. There is never a routine description of things.

We not only know what Willoughby cared for, but see how his dress and accessories are part of his charm for Marianne. Jane Austen's brilliant and solid chronicle of social objects goes beyond a psychological record, which fills the world with things in order to dramatise individual attitudes and appetites. She needs to make her discriminations for the purpose of a moral argument. Her presentation anticipates Henry James's more explicit insistence, made through Madame Merle's materialistic lecture to the romantic Isabel Archer, on the subject of expressive things:

'There's no such thing as an isolated man or woman; we're each of us made up of some cluster of appurtenances. What shall we call our "self"? Where does it begin? where does it end? It over-flows into everything that belongs to us – and then it flows back again. I know a large part of myself is in the clothes I choose to wear. I've a great respect for *things*! One's self – for other people – is one's expression of one's self; and one's house, one's furniture, one's garments, the books one reads, the company one keeps – these things are all expressive.' (*The Portrait of a Lady*, Chapter XIX)

Jane Austen shows the unpleasant possibilities of becoming too attached to things. She also knows that life in her society is inevi-tably lived with and through things. The people in her novels become restricted and even reified by living too much in the com-pany of objects. She shows how the object-stuff can flow back into the self or spirit through the things people care about and demand. Perhaps it is the moderated materialism of Mrs Jennings that allows her to put the matter in a nut-shell. She describes Miss Grey's price and Willoughby's values:

'Fifty thousand pounds, my dear. Did you ever see her? a smart, stilish girl they say, but not handsome. I remember her aunt very well, Biddy Henshawe; she married a very wealthy man. But the family are all rich together. Fifty thousand pounds! and by all accounts it won't come before it's wanted; for they say he is all to pieces. No wonder! dashing about with his curricle and hunters! Well, it don't signify talking, but when a young man, be he who he will, comes and makes love to a pretty girl, and promises marriage, he has no business to fly off from his word only because he grows poor, and a richer girl is ready to have him. Why don't he, in such a case, sell his horses, let his house, turn off his servants, and make a thorough reform at once?' (*S&S*, p. 194)

Jane Austen's knowledge and imagination go even beyond the assimilation of people to their properties. She shows how we relate to people through their accessories, how we can assimilate not only both object and person, but may attach ourselves to other people's property and properties. Marianne pretends to make romantically low demands, but actually wants a great deal. Her conventional and fashionable materialism is easily compatible with a self-centred and vague enthusiasm. Her demands pick up Willoughby's demands – as demands will. She starts wanting 'a carriage, perhaps two, and hunters' as well as music and books. Food for the mind mingles with food for the fancy, and some of her desires are merely glamorous. Jane Austen makes silly Mrs Bennet say that she still has a soft spot for a red coat, but she knows that it is not only fools who respond to each other in full social panoply. An eye for sexual colour and shape, for instance, tends to take in the aids to colour and shape, and so the reifications of love proceed. Marianne starts to fall in love with Willoughby:

> His manly beauty and more than common gracefulness were instantly the theme of general admiration, and the laugh which his gallantry raised against Marianne, received particular spirit from his exterior attractions. – Marianne herself had seen less of his person than the rest, for the confusion which crimsoned over her face, on his lifting her up, had robbed her of the power of regarding him after their entering the house. But she had seen enough of him to join in all the admiration of the others, and with an energy which always adorned her praise. His person and air were equal to what her fancy had ever drawn for the hero of a favourite story. . . . His name was good, his residence was in their favourite village, and she soon found out that of all manly dresses a shooting-jacket was the most becoming. (*S&S*, p. 43)

Willoughby's shooting-jacket is the becoming aid which helps to create his dashing 'manly' image. Like advertisers who blur the appeal of objects in the appeals of nature, Jane Austen knows how to create the conventional social and sexual stimulus for the weak, romantic susceptibility. After the shooting-jacket, Colonel Brandon's flannel waistcoat is naturally less appealing, in a society accustomed to correlate sex with health, sport and youth. Jane Austen's sense of the social determinations of our affective life seizes on the irresistible blend in an image approved by society and literature. Far from being tactless in dwelling on Colonel Brandon's twinges of rheumatism, she is strongly attacking the cosmetic element in sexual attraction. It might be an exaggeration to suggest that she anticipates Beckett's geriatric love-stories: she is scarcely marrying off Marianne to an old and impotent husband, as we may infer from her concluding comments on Brandon's recovery of tone, and the information that 'in time' Marianne came to love him as much as she had once loved Willoughby. 'In time' is a candid and searching phrase – it has taken Marianne time to lose the romantic image of appearance in the reality of experience. The romantic image itself thrives on instant response. In *Northanger Abbey* there is an analysis of materialism in which Catherine is redeemed, but where people tend to show either a harmless or a harmful attitude to the object-world, and hence to each other. *Sense and Sensibility* begins to recognise a more complex interaction of things and people. This interaction develops in *Pride and Prejudice*, where a heroine more intelligent than Marianne and more fallible than Elinor shows how wit and imagination can be entangled in appearances. In this novel Jane Austen seems to feel freer to admit that appearances may not always be irrelevant. Elinor and Marianne were matched with husbands of sterling quality, designed to defeat or outlive the dangers of charm and good looks. In *Pride and Prejudice* Jane Austen relaxes her rigour, admitting that outside and inside are at times appropriately matched. Elizabeth's liveliness and Darcy's elegance are charms which reflect mind and body. But there is enough rigour present to keep hero and heroine apart until they come to understand the nature of what they love. Darcy comes to admire Elizabeth, after first feeling no attraction. He is drawn by her fine eyes and also by her figure. But he cannot be allowed to possess her without understanding that love is not possession, and that her outside has not revealed her whole mind. But if he misreads, so does she. There is more to each than meets the eye. She first admires him – as she half-seriously tells Jane – in his image, which she first gazes at unabashed by physical presence, on the visit to Pemberley. His image is there in more ways than one.

Pemberley echoes the worthiness of Squire Allworthy's seat. Its beauties and prospects are seen through Elizabeth's eyes. The houses in *Pride and Prejudice* are nearly all taken for granted by the author because they are taken for granted by the characters, though environment is given some character by objects and habits.

As soon as the characters visit a new place, it is put before the reader. Elizabeth visits Charlotte Collins's new house and is immediately shown round. Mr Collins is a minute guide, self-gratified by possessions, liking to show Elizabeth what she has missed, fishing for praise, and inclined to unselective enumeration. He is the perfect cicerone for the visit to Rosings, and sense is submerged in his anxiety to put the other guests at their ease: 'I would advise you merely to put on whatever of your clothes is superior to the rest, there is no occasion for any thing more.' His way with things reflects Lady Catherine's more rational superiority: 'Lady Catherine will not think the worse of you for being simply dressed. She likes to have the distinction of rank preserved.' Rosings is introduced and described through Mr Collins's eyes, voice and values, enumerating 'the windows in front of the house' and relating 'what the glazing altogether had originally cost Sir Lewis De Bourgh' (pp. 161–2). The owner of Rosings resembles General Tilney in her appreciation of her guest's appreciation. She patronises through servants, plate and food, especially delighted 'when any dish on the table proved a novelty'. Every object in the drama of Lady Catherine's hospitality, including the fish used in the game of casino and the piano which she offers for Elizabeth's use, is a comic counter in the game of demand-and-supply which she plays so happily, best of all with Mr Collins, who is just the guest the hostess requires.

When Elizabeth comes to Pemberley, we not only see it through her eyes, but against the background of the visit to Rosings. Jane Austen manipulates those contrasts and parallels which form all fictions through the characters' sensibility. The plentiful and refreshing luncheon, elegantly presented, 'beautiful pyramids of grapes, nectarines, and peaches', and even the diffident and shy hospitality of Georgiana Darcy, are contrasted with the ostentation of Rosings. The handsome house is a sympathetic habitat in every way. Its saloon has a northern aspect which is cool in summer – Jane Austen is always attentive to temperature – and the sense of space is neither intimidating nor lofty. Like Allworthy's house, it partakes of the handsomeness and honesty of its owner:

It was a large, handsome, stone building, standing well on rising ground, and backed by a ridge of high woody hills; – and in front, a stream of some natural importance was swelled into greater, but without any artificial appearance. Its banks were neither formal, nor falsely adorned. Elizabeth was delighted. She had never seen a place for which nature had done more, or where natural beauty had been so little counteracted by an awkward taste. (*P&P*, p. 245)

Jane Austen makes her heroine appreciate the quality of the furnishings too, as 'suitable to the fortune of their proprietor' and his taste, 'neither gaudy nor uselessly fine', as she makes the contrast with Rosings. But Jane Austen does not make Elizabeth aware only of Darcy's property and taste. She responds also to a less definable quality in the atmosphere of the house, suggested by the variety and spaciousness. As Elizabeth goes over Pemberley, there is a sense of movement and exhilaration:

Every disposition of the ground was good; and she looked on the whole scene, the river, the trees scattered on its banks, and the winding of the valley, as far as she could trace it, with delight. As they passed into other rooms, these objects were taking different positions; but from every window there were beauties to be seen. (*P&P*, p. 246)

The vivid account of moving through a sequence of large rooms with large windows extending over wide vistas also conveys the heroine's elation. Outside and inside, Pemberley extends her acquaintance with Darcy, and in tangible or intangible ways it offers her a charm and a guarantee. Jane Austen is creating the spirit of a place.

Mansfield Park, like Northanger Abbey, resembles its owner. It is grand, large and daunting, and does not make Fanny feel at home: 'The grandeur of the house astonished, but could not console her. The rooms were too large for her to move in with ease; whatever she touched she expected to injure, and she crept about in constant terror of something or other' (*MP*, p. 14). Unlike Northanger, Mansfield is a neutral ground, which can be re-occupied and changed. In this novel, Jane Austen moves away from the simple equation of possessor and possessions to examine the home as a communal place.

As a home, Mansfield is imperfect. It does not put any of its children entirely at ease; its father is too remote and repressive, its mother too languid, letting responsibility pass into the mean and greedy hands of Mrs Norris, too indulgent and too harsh. (Indulgence and harshness are two sides of the same coin: Mrs Norris acts only for herself.) It is she who proposes the adoption of Fanny, her method being to work through the hospitality and generosity of others. She maintains an image at very little expense. It is she who organises the keeping-down of Fanny, whose unlit fire is warm enough for her until Sir Thomas comes to give her the warmth he has not known was lacking. Maria and Julia give her unwanted sashes and toys, her cousin Tom teases her and showers on her a profusion of work-boxes, her cousin Edmund gives her what she needs – until Mary Crawford comes to engross the new mare and more. Fanny, called 'creepmouse' by Tom, steals artlessly into a room of her own, and it becomes the only 'nest of comforts' in Mansfield Park. It is a room with a view, for the outward look of Fanny looks ahead to George Eliot's Dorothea Brooke and E. M. Forster's Lucy Honeychurch. Fanny looks beyond the indoor world of the drawing-room to the evening sky to gaze at those stars that are visible from the window, and longs to see those out of sight. We see the light infiltrating more indirectly into the East room, through 'a gleam of sunshine' and in the air she thinks of giving to her geraniums, while also inhaling 'a breeze of mental strength herself' (pp. 151–2). She collects the cast-off objects that can be cherished only by loving memory, and the room becomes the archive of Mansfield Park.

Every aspect of the room responds to the values of its occupant and her occupation. Unlike the drawing-room, which Mary Craw-ford's wit accurately describes as 'too hot', its low temperature rears a fragile life and makes it strong. The things in the room are harmonised by Fanny's capacity for love and acceptance, 'the whole . . . so blended together, so harmonized by distance, that every former affliction had its charm' (p. 152). The ability to use memory and imagination to include, and not exclude, is implicit in Fanny and Anne Elliot. It is an aspect of the self-knowledge which distin-guishes the rational passions of Fanny and Anne from the dissociated feelings of the Bertrams, the Crawfords and the Elliots. Fanny's life comes to have wholeness. Her nest of comforts also joins together the family things, creates a small warm space for herself at the heart of the house. Edmund's praise of her 'little establishment' is less playful and more promising than he knows.

For Mansfield Park lacks a heart and a centre. But it is not a static habitat, and its adopted child changes its shape and its atmosphere. It has, after all, taken her in. The spirit of the place is more sus-ceptible to improvement than Sotherton, and the novelist dwells on the emblem of Sotherton to show the greater mobility of Mansfield. We see Mansfield largely through Fanny's eyes, but we first hear the details of Sotherton from Edmund, who describes it to Mary Craw-ford when he sits next to her at dinner, as an Elizabethan house, 'a

large, regular, brick building – heavy, but respectable looking. . . .
It is ill-placed. It stands in one of the lowest spots of the park; in that
respect, unfavourable for improvement. But the woods are fine. . . .'
(p. 56). Mary realises that Edmund is making 'the best of it'. What
he says next applies to much more than his attitude to a house:
'. . . had I a place to new fashion, I should not put myself into the
hands of an improver. I would rather have an inferior degree of
beauty, of my own choice, and acquired progressively.'

On the 'improving' visit to Sotherton every aspect of house and
grounds is suggestive and the significances emerge and expand
through the viewpoints of the characters. The heavy opulence is all
too expressive of Mr Rushworth. Maria Bertram chooses him for his
property, and house and owner are almost interchangeable in their
inertness. On the visit to Sotherton Maria's elation is carefully evalu-
ated as 'a pleasure to increase with their approach to the capital free-
hold mansion, and ancient manorial residence of the family, with all
its rights of Court-Leet and Court-Baron' (p. 82). The cottages are
'a disgrace' but the church is fortunately 'not so close to the Great
House as often happens in old places' where 'the annoyance of the
bells must be terrible'. Like its owner, 'it is heavy, but respectable
looking'. 'The situation of the house excluded the possibility of much
prospect from any of the rooms' and every 'room on the west front
looked across a lawn to the beginning of the avenue immediately
beyond tall iron palisades and gates.' Its chapel is elegant, but no
longer used, and makes a good set for *double-entendres*. The pictures are abundant, 'and some few good, but the larger part were
family portraits, no longer any thing to any body but Mrs. Rushworth'. The family profiles in Fanny's room were thought of as being
unworthy to be anywhere but in her room: Mansfield has a better
curator than Sotherton.

When the members of the Mansfield party leave the house to go
over the grounds, Jane Austen goes beyond the symbolism of place
to make a theatre for many different responses and acts. The desire
to improve Sotherton is a specious excuse, the merest of alibis.
Instead of discussing improvements, they wander after each other to
suffer what Jane Austen calls 'cross accidents'. Henry Crawford sees
'walks of great promise'. Fanny is left alone on her bench in the
wilderness, while Mary and Edmund find their way to the avenue
she has longed to see. Maria squeezes dangerously through the gate
with Henry Crawford, unwilling to wait for Mr Rushworth, who has
forgotten to bring the key. She risks tearing her gown and falling

into the ha-ha, as warned by Fanny. Julia follows them, escaping
and pursuing. As Fanny sees Maria and Henry go off together,
'taking a circuitous, and as it appeared to her, very unreasonable
direction to the knoll, they were soon beyond her eye' (p. 100), it is
conspicuous as the single occasion when Henry and Maria move out
of sight of character and reader.

The house and grounds are designed for appropriate action,
though it is expressive rather than crucial. It is typical of Jane
Austen's matter-of-factness in symbolism, her merging of symbol in
surface. To call the Sotherton scene proleptic would be a tautology.
What is done in Sotherton is typically done, and the small-scale
action anticipates the later crisis and climax, because these too are
totally in character.

The only happy person on the expedition is Mrs Norris, who
characteristically carries off the booty she has 'spunged', the cream
cheese, beautiful little heath, and the pheasant's eggs which she is
going to get hatched by one of the maids at Mansfield (like Fanny).
The things Mrs Norris takes away are not hospitably presented but
acquired by her scrounging flatteries from the gardener and the
housekeeper. The things are part of the place, though they tell us
about the guests as well as the host and hostess. Every superficial
detail of the Sotherton visit, including the journey there and back,
contributes to a realistic account of a family visit, is deeply founded
in character, and therefore forms an organic part of the total
structure.

Other places and things develop in significance. Hospitality is
warmer at the Parsonage whose large round dining-table covered in
dishes is seen through the jealous disapproval of Mrs Norris. Its
hospitality is expressive of the childless Mrs Grant's spoiling of her
husband, whose good table eventually kills him. It is also, of course,
eloquent of his own indulgence, and the geese, turkeys and pheasants
play an important role in establishing character. But Mrs Grant,
like Fanny, does grow things and the evergreens in her shubbery
will last. Fanny rhapsodises on them, and Mary Crawford carelessly
admits that they do very well for a village parsonage.

The Parsonage contains its visitors, Mary and Henry Crawford,
and its elegance and hospitality are pressed into symbolic service as
Edmund becomes charmed by Mary:

A young woman, pretty, lively, with a harp as elegant as herself;
and both placed near a window, cut down to the ground, and

opening on a little lawn, surrounded by shrubs in the rich foliage of summer, was enough to catch any man's heart. The season, the scene, the air, were all favourable to tenderness and sentiment. Mrs. Grant and her tambour frame were not without their use; it was all in harmony; and as every thing will turn to account when love is once set going, even the sandwich tray, and Dr. Grant doing the honours of it, were worth looking at. (p. 65)

There is a quiet but definite approximation of the woman to place and object, appropriate to Mary's assimilation to a surface of richness and ease, and to Edmund's response to appearances. As General Tilney is assimilated to his possessions by putting too much vital energy into them, and using them to manipulate other people until they begin to be an inseparable aspect of self, so Mary's genuine vitality and intelligence are endangered. She struggles against the assimilation by her environment, but it has been going on for too long, and she cannot escape. Edmund progresses to 'acquire' his 'inferior beauty', who is superior in many ways.

Hospitality and donation become more prominent in *Mansfield Park*. If Fanny brings warmth and strength to Mansfield Park, she has also drawn warmth and strength from its hospitality, and from its presents which she treasures as sacred objects. She has been taught by Edmund, who first gave her the things that human beings need for love and growth: writing materials to write to her brother, the new mare for healthy exercise, books for the mind, wine for her aching head, a chain for her cross. She has to learn to give as well as to receive, and a step in her education is marked when she heals a family wound by making Betsy a present of a silver knife. Sir Thomas is capable of good giving too (a home, a fire and a gown), and even Lady Bertram tries to lend her maid and offers a prospective puppy. Mrs Norris does not give a present to her god-child, Betsy. She gives one present, the mysterious 'something considerable' to William, which the reader knows from internal evidence is less than the ten pounds given him by Lady Bertram, and the exact amount of which was revealed by Jane Austen to her family. She was as aware as Henry James of the occasional need for not specifying things.

Mansfield Park contains enough good things given to Fanny, to be animated by memory and love, and returned in her gratitude and growth. For Mansfield Park does nourish its adopted child. She in her turn adopts the East room for her own. The major act of hospitality brings in an outsider to strengthen and sweeten the community. Jane Austen makes it clear, however, that the good giving and good taking are dependent on considerable purchasing-power. Fanny and Edmund are not materialists, but they are fully provided with material comforts.

In *Mansfield Park*, the sympathetic habitat is most developed, but also most open. It is as if the simpler moral associations of places were there most thoroughly expressed, and a limit reached. Sotherton and Portsmouth are simple habitats. The rooms, food, woods and gardens of Mansfield Park, and even the exterior and interior of Mansfield Parsonage – which is, after all, to be inherited by Fanny and Edmund – are dramatised more variously to embody hopes for harmony and for change. After *Mansfield Park* it is not surprising that Jane Austen moves away from the houses to the significance of smaller and more shifting things.

In *Emma* hospitality and donation become prominent themes. Everyone is a guest, some are hosts and guests. Everyone either gives or takes, some do both. Jane Austen's implicit analysis of social rela-tionships depends on objects as on groups. Human beings create for themselves a social case or cover composed of things, and relate to each other through more movable objects. The prominent hosts in the novel are Mr Woodhouse, Mr Weston and Mr Knightley. Mr Woodhouse is generous within the bounds of his own narrow imagination, egocentrically fastidious and hypochondriacal. Mr Weston's generosity is harmlessly over-hospitable, and his good wine does no more than precipitate Mr Elton's proposal to Emma. Mr Knightley's sense of propriety is entirely approved by his author, but he makes it plain to Mrs Elton that the hospitality of Donwell Abbey cannot be delegated.

Hospitality is a form of giving and taking, and blends with the theme of donation. Benefactors benefit themselves and the people to whom they give. Emma and her father give generously to Miss Bates and Mrs Bates – 'I sent them the whole hind-quarter' – but it is easier to give things than a proper attention. It serves Emma right when Jane Fairfax sends back her arrowroot. Jane has had to accept too many benefactions and it is good that she rebels. She is beset by treacherous objects, like Frank's piano and his letters, Mr Perry's carriage and the alphabet game. The carefully named 'Frank' has better luck with Mrs Bates's broken spectacles, and having fastened the rivet 'was very warmly thanked both by mother and daughter'. Emma is a clever manipulator of objects too, and uses charades, her picture, and a broken shoe-lace, to help on her match-making for Harriet and Mr Elton. Mr Knightley's things are like him. The last of the best baking apples and his strawberries are good and generously given. Miss Bates is good at accepting presents, unlike Mrs Elton who tires of strawberries in one half hour's talk.

The ordinary world animates things through people, and people through things. Things take a hand in human destiny. Donation is only one form of communicating feeling through objects. Mr Weston's good wine raises Mr Elton's ardour and a secluded carriage on a snowy night perfects the scene. Emma's reading-lists are more admirable than her reading, and Mr Knightley's preservation of one of them should alert us to his feelings. Mr Woodhouse's story about his grandson asking for a bit of string and his distress over the open air in Harriet's portrait – despite her shawl, – are endearing indexes of his triviality. Robert Martin's parlour, with the singing shepherd, promises well for Harriet's marriage, as do the walnuts he picks and the books he reads for her sake. His mother's present of the very fine goose to Mrs Goddard adds substance to her prospects. Mrs Elton's finery and Jane Fairfax's neat elegance are appropriate shells, the one fussy, the other restrained. These people need their survival kits, resembling other people inside and outside novels in needing or wanting to enlarge their powers, good or bad, with the aid of things.

In *Northanger Abbey, Sense and Sensibility,* and *Pride and Prejudice* there is a prevailing possessiveness. People clutch, hoard and acquire. In *Persuasion* the men and women are remembered through their possessions, but there is less emphasis on property. Dramatic properties are vital: Sir Walter Elliot has his Baronetage, his Gowland, and his room full of mirrors. (Admiral Croft turns most of them out.) The great parlour at Uppercross has the modern pianoforte (presumably replacing a harpsichord), and a disarray of little tables imported by the new generation, Louisa and Henrietta.

Captain Wentworth has his ships, and talks about his first command, the *Asp,* with a fine sense of objects and audience when he compares it with an old pelisse for the benefit of the female listeners. We are told that Anne has loved his wit, and Jane Austen conveys this wit through his not too serious manipulations of simile and emblem. A wit which has been exhibitionist in Mary Crawford is given a certain solidity in Captain Wentworth through his not too portentous play with actual objects as sources for imagery. He has a sense of the object, but also a sense of the artifice of using emblems.

He speaks with playful solemnity as he holds up the nut and uses it as an image for Louisa's firmness. He is right not to sound too serious – it is an inaccurate symbol, because he says it is unlike its 'brethren' who 'have fallen, and been trodden underfoot' (*P*, p. 88). Anne's objects are sacred ones, like Fanny's, but presented less conspicuously. She is willing to cut down on possessions, as her father and sister are not, finding it easier to leave their ancestral home than to retrench. When Mary asks Anne a resonant question which goes beyond its immediate occasion, 'Dear me! What can *you* possibly have to do?', she gives a brief account of her management of things: making a duplicate of the catalogue of books and pictures, arranging the destination of Elizabeth's plants, and arranging her own 'little concerns, books and music'. The impedimenta of a cultivated human being are modestly but clearly brought in, as with Fanny's nest of comforts in *Mansfield Park*.

The course of true love is strewn with objects. In *Persuasion* they are unobtrusive but numerous. At Lyme Regis, Anne's perceptive eye registers character in the Harvilles' lodgings, 'so small as none but those who invite from the heart could think capable of accommodating so many. Anne had a moment's astonishment on the subject herself. . . .' She compares their hospitality 'from the heart' with 'the usual style of give-and-take invitations', depressed by the lost past: 'These would have been all my friends' (p. 98). The rooms are small, but contain significant objects, which include 'the ingenious contrivances and nice arrangements of Captain Harville', who is one of the very few people in these novels who ever makes anything. Mrs Smith's charitable knick-knacks are also exceptional. Good food is made by servants, plants are occasionally grown, but most of the middle-class manufacture is amateur and utterly useless needlework, like Lady Bertram's carpetwork and endless fringe, or signs of accomplishment, like Charlotte Palmer's landscape in coloured silks, 'proof of her having spent seven years at a great school in town to some effect' (*S&S*, p. 160). Harville's craftmanship is characteristic of the man – he is a sailor, ingenious and constructive, making the most of small spaces. The things are products of his industry, and also relics of his voyages – 'some few articles of a rare species of wood, excellently worked up, and with something curious and valuable from all the distant countries'.

Anne's imagination, like Fanny's, is far-ranging. She is granted a more sophisticated sense of environment than any earlier heroine, even participating in her author's interest in 'the effect of professional influence on personal habits'. Anne is also moved, not altogether pleasurably, by 'the picture of repose and domestic happiness', a vicarious enjoyment her author had sharply imagined. Jane Austen never shows love in a cottage, but this is the nearest we come to it. Anne's enjoyment of the riches in the Harvilles' small room in spite of the 'common necessaries provided by the owner, in the common indifferent light' is a counter-balance to Fanny's distaste for the small rooms, unkempt furniture, loud noise and indifferent food of her parents' home in Portsmouth. Fanny comes to appreciate the elegancies and proprieties of Mansfield even more than before, though not quite as her uncle intends when he contrives his experiment in environment. What she yearns for is all that may be understood by the sense of home, including its people, 'her uncle's woods and her aunt's gardens', and all its imperfections. It takes Portsmouth to make Mansfield a home. Anne too has a sense of home, and like Fanny's it is not proprietorial. Anne has to vacate her home too, and Jane Austen draws our attention to her detachment. She shows a moment's imaginative temptation when Lady Russell invokes the image of her being mistress of Kellynch. She comes to admit to herself that 'Kellynch Hall had passed into better hands than its owners'. But she has also glimpsed, in the Harvilles' lodgings, a life that has nothing to do with great estates or rich possessions.

The objects in the Harvilles' room summon up a thought of an alternative life, remote and desirable. But as her fortunes recover, and she comes to think that Captain Wentworth 'must love her', there are a few obstacles. On their first encounter in Bath, Captain Wentworth offers her the hospitality of his new umbrella, but she is pre-engaged to walk with her cousin, in her thick boots, thicker than Mrs Clay's. In the concert hall Mr Elliot interrupts a promising conversation with Captain Wentworth by interposing the concert bill and asking her 'to explain Italian again'. In the hotel rooms which are animated for us by Anne's sense of comings and goings – 'a quick-changing, unsettled scene. One five minutes brought a note, the next a parcel' – Elizabeth Elliot 'pointedly' gives Captain Wentworth the card for her evening party, 'Miss Elliot at home'. In the same bustle Captain Harville shows her Captain Benwick's picture, and the ensuing debate encourages Captain Wentworth to write his letter to Anne. The object-filled world is all about them as Captain Wentworth pretends to have forgotten his gloves in order to take out his letter 'from under the scattered paper' and place it before Anne. Her agitation makes Mrs Musgrove order a chair, but a chair will 'never do', since it will make her 'lose the possibility of meeting Captain Wentworth'. Her brother-in-law Charles, who has a sporting humour, sacrifices his 'engagement at a gunsmith's' to escort her home, but when they meet Captain Wentworth he asks him to take his place so that he can go off to see 'a capital gun' which the gunsmith is keeping unpacked 'to the last possible moment': 'By his description it is a good deal like the second hand double-barrel of mine which you shot with one day, round Winthrop' (p. 240). Separated by so many things, the lovers are finally brought together with the help of gloves and guns. Human beings have to make the best of the objects to hand. Jane Austen's world is full of small objects as well as symbols, and they are often arbitrary and accidental.

The objects in *Persuasion*, as in the other novels, serve plot, animate action, define characters and give a solid sense of the world. They also seem to be present in greater and freer abandon in this novel, lying around, as objects do, in a casual clutter as part of the ordinary scenes and surfaces of life. Jane Austen occasionally uses objects as symbolic, like the ha-ha in *Mansfield Park*, or the autumn fields in *Persuasion*, but her touch with symbols is very delicate.

Accessory objects in *Persuasion* are often introduced with a fine carelessness, simply to give her people things to handle or look at while they think, feel or talk. On the occasion of the Elliot's evening party, which is 'but a card-party', the lovers, who don't play cards, meet, part, and meet again. They are relaxed and at ease together at last, even in the social scene. The environment seems stirred and brilliantly lit by Anne's radiance, but there is an absence of description and all the emphasis is placed within. As Anne and Captain Wentworth meet for one conversation, Jane Austen gives them 'a fine display of greenhouse plants' to admire. It is an occasion and a cover for the private exchange of memories. The object itself, though fine, green and natural, is wholly inert. When George Eliot brings Stephen Guest and Maggie Tulliver together in a conservatory, the colours and scents of the plants create a sensuous atmosphere and symbol. But Jane Austen, moved less by a symbolic urge than by a sense of appropriateness, simply chooses something which will give a sufficient sense of place and gesture for the conversation of love.

The author's dramatic self-effacement shows itself in her handling of things and places as much as in the handling of words. The novels are full of encounters with objects, significant or casual. Objects may be present but are sparingly described. The hyacinths in *Northanger Abbey* are given neither a colour nor a space; the greenhouse plants are fine, but of no particular species. Objects may assert themselves, if people need them, as accessories, relics or personal emblems, but are sometimes kept in their place, as objects in a background. The reality of her social scenes, especially in *Persuasion*, depends strongly on the casual presences of objects.

Such presences suggest that Jane Austen might have understood Robbe-Grillet's sense of the world and things:[2]

> The world is neither significant nor absurd. It *is*, quite simply. That, in any case, is the most remarkable thing about it. ... Around us, defying the noisy pack of our animistic or protective adjectives, things *are there*. Their surfaces are distinct and smooth, *intact*, neither suspiciously brilliant nor transparent. All our literature has not yet succeeded in eroding their smallest corner, in flattening their slightest curve.

NOTES

1 This essay is a slightly altered version of Chapter vi of my book *A Reading of Jane Austen*, published by Peter Owen (London, 1975) and New York University Press (New York, 1975), and is reproduced by permission of the publishers.

2 *For a New Novel: Essays on Fiction*, trans. Richard Howard (New York, 1965) p. 19. Originally published as *Pour un nouveau roman* (Paris, 1963).

6 Jane Austen: Poet

GEORGE WHALLEY

I must confess to a little uneasiness. Except for a long-standing, slow-burning admiration for Jane Austen's writing, for 'the achieve of, the mastery of the thing', I have nothing much to guide me. I have not even written a book on Jane Austen; so who can say where I stand in the critical spectrum, between the ultra-violet Janeites and the infra-red Austenists? There is, I know, a vast ocean of scholarship and criticism, puff-cheeked and sea-monster-haunted, in which Jane's work swims; but I have not studied the *Sailing Directions* that could have warned me of the sly currents and deceptive landfalls, and have neglected the *Notices to Mariners* with their record of the latest wrecks, the unlighted lights, the demolished seamarks, the unswept mine-fields. I feel like one who has been bidden to dine in the Captain's Room at Lloyd's, having no gold ring in the ear. But I recall that Jane had two naval brothers, that she admired both of them very much, and that both became admirals even though they had had less first-hand acquaintance with Pacific Island cannibals than Fanny Burney's midshipman brother had; and pray therefore for the impassivity of Joshua Slocum who – after his chronometer had gone over the side and his goat had eaten his charts – completed his voyage around the world alone, with no navigational aids beyond an alarm clock and a map torn from a school atlas.

I have, however, tried a little to see whether anybody else thought Jane Austen was a poet; but in vain. I had high hopes of one recent book that had distilled from all known critical approaches a multi-planal technique of analysis that would provide the last word – or almost the last word – on *Mansfield Park*. I peeped inside, but most of what I saw was about Marx and Freud and sociology, which I found unnecessarily distasteful. So I closed that book, and turned to Mr Southam's ingenious collection called *The Critical Heritage*. There I found a letter written by George Henry Lewes to Charlotte

Brontë in 1848; this seemed a little closer to the mark. Defending Jane Austen as 'one of the greatest artists ... that ever lived', Lewes went on to say, (a little incautiously, as it turned out) that 'Miss Austen is not a poetess, has no "sentiment", ... no eloquence, none of the ravishing enthusiasm of poetry'. Charlotte replied with proper indignation: 'Can there be a great artist without poetry? What I call ... a great artist ... cannot be destitute of the divine gift. But by *poetry*, I am sure, you understand something different to what I do'. It is not easy to see what Lewes meant here by 'poetry'; he says it is what Shakespeare had, and that in place of that we must put Jane Austen's 'daring prose'. But Miss Brontë is not much more lucid: poetry, she says, is passion and rapture, a power so divine that it had elevated George Sand's coarse masculinity and had been able to convert Thackeray's 'corrosive poison into purifying elixir'.[1] Having no acquaintance with corrosive poisons and very little with coarse masculinity, I have had to search my own heart; for Richard Simpson has said emphatically that Jane is no poet, and even Miss Lascelles, in declaring that Jane was no symbolist, may have meant that in her view too Jane was no poet.

Most of what we have of Jane Austen's verse is a sort of polished doggerel, and was not intended to be anything else; even when she came to utter her grief at the untimely death of Anne Lefroy, a niece beloved and almost as gifted as Jane herself, the verse, though noble in sentiment, is flat and rhetorical in execution – in the undesirable sense it is at once too 'poetical' and too 'prosaic'. Perhaps those who have said that Jane was no poet dismissed as of no serious account what (if anything) they knew of her verse, and could find in her novels none of those Icarus-passages of opulent emotive prose that sometimes get printed in italics, nor anything haunted (as Dickens sometimes is) by the submerged run of the blank verse line or the sonorous rhythms of the Authorised Version of the Bible. Nevertheless, I should still like to suggest that Jane Austen *is* a poet.

Jane Austen is supremely a writer of prose. As Coleridge knew, and Wordsworth echoed, the antithesis of prose is not poetry, but verse; the antithesis of poetry is science. Yeats's tone-deafness steered him away from the contemporary cult of trying to write 'musical' verse, and brought him to an unmatched sense of the integrity of language – significant words rhythmically disposed, passionate hieratic utterance keyed to the inventive rhythms of the speaking voice. In the same way, Jane Austen's incapacity for composing strong or eloquent verse seems to have endowed her with an incorruptible sense of the integrity of prose, the translucent rhythms of the speaking voice in the other harmony, the peculiar signature of breath and intelligence that identifies a person speaking and the state of mind that from moment to moment informs the voice. Miss Lascelles noticed that in some of Jane Austen's prose there is 'an impression of speed and simplicity not alien from the temper of verse.'[2] Her ear gave her an accurate intuition; I wish she had carried the hint a little further. If we reject the proposition that Jane Austen is a poet, we might be tempted to accept the doctrine that she is some sort of scientist – a microscopically objective recorder of a limited range of human behaviour; a very odd thing to say of a writer whose work is rather like Mozart, without the *Requiem.*

I am impressed by the fact that Jane Austen's characters are autonomous to such a degree that they have in our minds a life of their own, so that we can discuss them with great patience and refinement of perception – and with very little quarrelling – as though they were living persons (which of course they are). That she was able to do that was a marvellous achievement; and that it should be so accounts, I suppose, for the inexhaustible pleasure we find in talking to each other about her people, confident that any obtuseness or lack of a delicate insight on our part will be corrected by the real presence of the persons themselves as we discover and rediscover them in our reading. But I have a suspicion (reinforced by Professor Hardy's theme and by some of the things Professor Litz has said) that her achievement is even more remarkable than that, and feel that we should try to search out the compass of it – difficult though that may be when the achievement is apparently effortless, and the products of it have an impervious seamlessness.

I should like to suggest that Jane Austen is a poet in two senses: (a) in her craftsmanship in language; and (b) in the conduct of the action within each novel. In the first sense, we need to consider fine-grained detail with an ear alert to the dynamics of language; in the second, we are concerned with the disposition of forces within the whole universe of a novel, particularly that mutual definition of plot and character the product of which Aristotle called *drama*, the thing done, or what I may elsewhere – to distinguish it from the 'action' that is sheer motion – also call 'pure action'; the one sense discloses itself on a small scale, the other on a large scale. The evidence for each is of a particular kind, each different from the other. Yet both kinds or functions interact upon each other and can be seen to be poetic because both reside at the heart, or at the roots, of imaginative activity.

I shall not evolve my argument according to the convention that pretends that the conclusion follows necessarily from the evidence. The conclusion of a critical argument is always implicit in the premises, and in the selection and ordering of evidence that the premises direct. So I beg your indulgence to begin (as Aristotle says) 'with first things' – in this case with what I mean by 'poet', 'poetry', and 'imagination'. What I now have to say may be a bit dense, but I'll do the best I can with a topic too simple to be anything but unmanageable. The fact that Jane Austen may not have thought of these things in this way is, I think, neither here nor there.

I take it that imagination is not a 'faculty', but rather an integrated and potent state of the self – a *realising* condition, in which the self and the world are made real. I take it, correspondingly, that the word 'poetry' refers basically to a state of language, a condition qualitatively discernible but not analytically definable – or not yet; a state of language that is noticeably lucid, vivid, nervous, inventive, economical, often translucent, capable of swift movement. Incorrigibly a matter of words (and not dominantly of musical sounds), poetry is informed – or declares itself – by the inventive rhythms of a mind unfolding what cannot be known except in the uttering of it. The rhythms and tone are the indelible marks of energy and of the quality of impulse. To put it another way: poetry is language in the process of symbolising. By 'symbolising' I do not mean so much that poetry typically produces 'symbols' – those distinguishable images that tiresomely invite us to prodigies of allegorical exposition; rather, that 'symbolising' generates (or simply *is*) 'symbolic events', verbal events that are strongly resonant, in which words tend to assume tactual qualities and complex – even contradictory – upper partials of implication. Under the condition of poetry, language becomes 'musicalised'; it discovers – without renouncing the integrity of language – something like the condition of music, showing typically (as language otherwise seldom does) a capacity for swift unprepared change, modulation, variation, transition, and also a capacity for stillness and composure. In this state the logic of thought and grammar is not necessarily dismissed, but language tends to gravitate to a more primitive state, having an active commerce with the senses, and relying upon the intrinsic relations of collision and parataxis (the metaphorical function) and the pure physical interaction of the elements of language as spoken and listened to. 'Symbolising' is the antithesis of 'describing'; 'describing' is language in a scientific mode.

A 'poet', then, may be seen not simply as a manufacturer of verses, or of magniloquent strings of words, but – if we may trust the Greek root of the word – a *maker*, and specifically a maker in words. The art of poetry is a rather physical and forthright business, not devoid of intelligence, but having much to do with craftsmanship and the craftsman's respect for his materials. The gift is a supremely human one, not divine (except as far as some would hold that all our gifts are of divine origin). We are not actually capable of *creating*; we select and arrange what is given to us (though the source may be obscure or totally unknown); a poet allows and encourages promising elements – words and rhythms usually – to assume form, to move in an ordered manner. On the whole, the more intense the poetry, the less mellifluous it is. As David Jones has said, a poet has to use what is around the place, and he can make true poetry only of what he knows and loves. The need to know makes a poet an accurate and patient observer; his love prevents his knowing from stopping short in description. 'Naming' – the affectionate telling over of things as a liturgy of wonder – is one of the richest subordinate resources of poetry.

A novelist needs a talent for telling a story that a lyrical poet does not need; and his choice of the harmony of prose, and the lengths that prose may drive him to, make demands on him that an epic poet, or perhaps even a writer of formal history, would not encounter. Yet whatever imaginative universe the novelist may encompass or seek to encompass, the reality and command of it will stand or fall by the quality of his making, and the quality of his wording. The whole thing has to be made in words – not least the characters. The 'better' the wording – that is, the more exactly proper to what in the end proves to have been necessary – the more the novel becomes (like a poem) self-subsistent and self-declarative, depending least upon the person of the novelist even though it must all occur in his mind and will be coloured by it; and probably depending very little upon the author's personal wounds and longings. But language is an unruly servant, especially if roughly handled, being no passive instrument. In the end it will have its way of all imperious masters, will stick out an impish tongue at whatever orotund spaces in the rhetoric it has been forced to set echoing, and at any emotional overindulgence it has been obliged to collude in. Good writing, of whatever kind, seems always to have come into existence as its own utterance, speaking in a conceivable voice, finding its wording as an act of grace. If I think of a novelist as a 'poet', I think of one (certainly) who lives in an imaginative universe that is rooted in life and the ways of human life; but his universe is also haunted by words, shaped by utterances. If these seem large claims, Jane Austen may be allowed her say – even though it comes from an early book and a hilarious setting.

'And what are you reading, Miss ——?' 'Oh! it is only a novel!' replies the young lady; while she lays down her book with affected indifference, or momentary shame. – 'It is only Cecilia, or Camilla, or Belinda;' or, in short, only some work in which the greatest powers of the mind are displayed, in which the most thorough knowledge of human nature, the happiest delineation of its varieties, the liveliest effusions of wit and humour are conveyed to the world in the best chosen language. (*NA*, p. 38)

Jane Austen, as far as I know, made no claim for herself as a poet: and I am not trying to show that she was something that she had no idea of being. My concern is simply to allow us to enter into the unique universes of her imagining, and to dwell there if we wish. There would certainly be some danger in expanding the concept of poetry to embrace everything effectively conducted in words (? Newton's *Principia Mathematica*, for example). But the danger of extending 'poetry' some way into the usually acknowledged realm of prose seems to me easier to accept than the distortions that occur when we try to define the novel as though it were absolutely distinct from all other imaginative makings-in-words. Many have called Jane Austen a great artist; I have no quarrel with that. But 'artist' is an elusive term, and 'poet' – if we insist on the word's having an indissoluble connection with language – may serve us better in trying to draw a bounding line around the specific qualities of Jane Austen's work.

That should provide some sort of setting for the first sense of the word 'poet'. Now, to take a fresh nip and consider the second sense.

Whateley, Macaulay, and Lewes, all at an early date, ascribed to Jane Austen an exceptional flair for drawing characters, for discriminating them one from another, and presenting them 'dramatically' – that is, in speaking-parts; the 'fools' (or 'noodles', as Lewes liked to call them) they found especially praiseworthy, as though they somehow served a function only loosely connected with the novels in which they found themselves.³ So impressed were they with Jane Austen's ability in drawing characters that they said it was 'Shakespearean', and Lewes called her a 'Prose Shakespeare'. Richard Simpson, himself a Shakespearean scholar, courteously noticed that it was Heywood who had some time earlier been called the 'Prose Shakespeare', but he agreed that 'Miss Austen much more really deserves the title.' Lewes however had reservations – Jane Austen, he said, sometimes speaks 'through the *personae*', she lacks passion, she has no interest in the picturesque. Simpson had reservations too: 'within her range her characterization is truly Shakespearian; but she has scarcely a spark of poetry.'⁴ Having made an important observation, they let the virtue of it slip through their fingers: they seem to have said no more than that at character-drawing she is very good indeed, almost as good as Shakespeare, but of course she really is not so big or grand or poetical as he was – and she did write in prose, you know. If her 'Shakespearean' quality is to be taken as a specific indication, we can give it more point by noticing what Coleridge found impressive about Shakespeare. He rejoiced as much as anybody else in the variety and life-likeness of Shakespeare's characters, and marvelled at the copiousness of his invention. But two things that struck him just as forcibly were these: that none of Shakespeare's characters seemed in any way a projection of Shakespeare himself, and were not drawn naturalistically from the life; and that Shakespeare was never guilty of 'ventriloquism', of speaking deceptively through his characters in his own person. These, I am sure, are also specific qualities in Jane Austen, and we have taken a step forward.

Again, it is a pity to let the just claim for Jane Austen's 'dramatic' power dissolve into no more than a statement that she could call forth a wide variety of life-like characters and let them talk themselves into existence. Certainly she did that – triumphantly – but what else? Edwin Muir, in his account of the kind of novel he calls 'dramatic', takes us a long step forward, not least because here he is writing about Jane Austen and not about Shakespeare.

There is in her novels, in the first place, a confinement to one circle, one complex of life, producing naturally an intensification of action; and this intensification is one of the essential attributes of the dramatic novel. In the second place, character is to her no longer a thing merely to delight in. ... It has consequences. It influences events; it creates difficulties and later, in different circumstances, dissolves them. ... The balance of all the forces within the novel creates and moulds the plot. There is no external framework, no merely mechanical plot; all is character, and all is at the same time action. ...

Where this plot [in *Pride and Prejudice*] differs from the plot of a novel of action is in its strict interior causation. ... The correspondence in a novel of this kind between the action and the characters is so essential that one can hardly find terms to describe it without appearing to exaggerate; one might say that a change in the situation always involves a change in the characters, while every change, dramatic or psychological, external or internal, is either caused or given its form by something in both.[5]

This account of Jane Austen's procedure sounds very much like a direct application of Aristotle's view of tragedy to the conduct of prose fiction. The sources of individual action are internal; a man becomes what he does; the plot is a function of the characters, the characters are continuously changed by the plot but also determine it; the overt plot and the characters – what is done by whom, to whom, and why – is not the end (or purpose) of the piece but an aspect of what defines the intricate and finely traced arc of pure action, allows the configuration of action to be traced out in physically discernible and humanly intelligible terms. Aristotle's view of tragedy is dynamic and radical; there is nothing in it to support the weak behaviourist assumption of a 'tragic flaw'; there is no place in it for the arbitrary intervention of the gods of fate; it is inflexibly human; the protagonist is *not* called a 'hero'; least of all does the *Poetics* itself support the notion that Aristotle provided (as the Italians seem to have thought and as many thoughtless instructors continue to suppose) a checklist of the required ingredients for cooking a tragedy. In any case, a cockpit check tells us whether it is safe to fly; it does not tell us that we are flying, or how well. Aristotle emphatically and repeatedly affirms the indivisible dynamic relation between plot and character. In the fragmentary form in which the *Poetics* has come down to us, he pays much more attention to plot than to character – not because he was thinking of a kind of play different from Shakespeare's or from ours, but because he saw both plot and character as operating as instrumental rather than as an end. His central perception was of an action – a *drama*, a 'pure action' – that plot and character together delineate: the *drama* traced out by the whole play was what made tragedy specifically tragic.

What he had to say about the specific *drama* of comedy is lost to us, but that doesn't bother me much at the moment.

To those of us who are in the habit of thinking of the 'action' in a novel or play or film as the overt (and preferably sensational) things that the people do or have done to them, the internality of Aristotle's view of the nature and sources of tragedy will probably seem a bit esoteric. But Aristotle's view of dramatic action is all of a piece with his ethical view of the sources of human action. And Coleridge, in all his reflections upon moral and dramatic values, also insists upon the internality, the self-originating nature, of action; we cannot without damage go behind the statement 'I act'; it is always an 'I' acting, decisively and irreversibly; restraint from action can therefore be an act. He is acutely aware of the bond between action and passion, between doing and being done to, and of the correlation of action and passion in any one person. That actions are literally coloured by what informs them – be it will, desire, impulse, or lyrical self-realisation – he is in no doubt; and it is upon these axioms of the nature of human action that his judgement of plays and novels (among many other things) turns; on these grounds he chose Fielding above Richardson, and admired *Tom Jones* as inordinately as anybody ever has. For Coleridge, as I am sure would be the case for Jane Austen if she ever ventured into philosophical discourse, 'moral' and 'aesthetic' are not mutually exclusive terms; he remembered that the root of the word 'aesthetics' is not 'beauty' or 'artistic form', but 'feeling' and 'perception'. If Coleridge sometimes gets into difficulties with the exposition of these intangible home-truths, it is largely because he rejected the whole regressive logic of 'motives', 'drives', and compulsions; like Aristotle he saw 'cause' in the fulfilment of the end. It may take a little effort to adopt a non-behavioural view of character and plot, but I think that we are ill-advised not to try.

As a preliminary proposition, then, I suggest that Jane Austen's novels can fruitfully be regarded as 'poems', in some such sense as I have already unfolded. As long as a novel is considered to be a genuine imaginative construction, the 'fictions' of the novel – whether the doings and happenings, the episodes, places or persons – will be apprehended as 'real' rather than actual, as of universal rather than general import; and we shall expect to see fictional particulars transformed (through the virtue of their particularity) into aspects of universal human values. The test of 'reality' is not whether the episodes and persons represent – or could conceivably represent – actual events and persons, but whether the symbolic transformation into real persons and places and events occurs or not. (Plausibility is a matter of internal judgement, not of sociological generalisation.) Symbolic transformation, I suppose, occurs in the author's mind; but it must occur in physical terms in the body of the book, in the wording and ordonnance of it and not simply in what the words depict. What the actors can be seen to do and suffer is not the end or purpose of the writing, firmly though the actors may command our attention; these are the physical aspects of what allows the arc of pure action, the *drama*, to be traced out in a discernible manner.

Jane Austen was evidently a conscious, perceptive, and highly skilled craftsman: in her work, in spite of her exuberance, nothing seems ever to depend upon accident or improvisation; her writing, like her most memorable young ladies, is clear-eyed and of a fine complexion. She said herself, playfully but truly, that 'An artist cannot do anything slovenly' (*Letters*, p. 30). She found her mastery by choosing firm foundations for her style and by writing a great deal from the age of fifteen onward, first of all writing for her family, an audience that shared her sense of fun. From very early on, when she was writing she was listening, judging, refining, attuning, until her pen – which she was incapable of handling clumsily – responded, with the sensitiveness of a gold-leaf electrometer, to that fertile indirection of the mind that (at a loss for terms) we sometimes call 'imagination', and sometimes 'thought', and sometimes 'intention'. Among the six novels that she published there is no performance that can justly be called juvenile or tentative.

The first sense in which Jane Austen's writing can be seen as 'poetic', her verbal craftsmanship or wordsmithery (her particular achievement being of the order of what Coleridge called 'logodae-daly' or 'sleight of words'), falls within the field of what is usually called 'style'. Her style has been examined perceptively by more than one scholar, but not (I think) definitively; and to think of her as a poet is bound to put a sharper and more selective edge than has been customary upon the inquiry into her style.

In saying that Jane Austen is a 'poet' in her handling of words, I do not mean that she writes continuously in a manner that we should agree was noticeably 'poetic'. She has at her disposal the full scope of prose, from plain factual narrative and description to the most refined resources of tone, implication, allusive nuance, pace, and emphasis. None of this falls outside the theoretical limits of poetry –

if we accept for 'poetry' post-Johnsonian criteria that Jane Austen herself might not have had consciously in mind. Being a poet, she reserves the privilege of making her language 'poetical' only when it needs to be; writing in prose, and not insisting to herself that she is a poet, she has the immense advantage of not feeling all the time on her shoulders the oppressive weight of singing-robes. And yet, even though her language may not be always and recognisably 'musicalised', it seems always to be on the fringes of the musical, capable of moving in and out of the musical state with an effortless rapidity that we associate with the musical state itself. Having established for herself a very small range of rhetorical effects, the slightest variation of tone, pace, or activity is immediately noticeable; and we become aware of an undercurrent of verbal possibilities that – breaking the surface and disappearing again – engage us with shocks of delight and recognition. For example, we have the general impression that the staple of Jane Austen's prose is the short, crisp, translucent sentence; but she is no Hemingway. The length and structure of her sentences adapt themselves instantly to local and particular need; whether it is the sinewy suppleness of syntax that can embrace the exact shade of an ironic aside or the lizard-turn of an epigram; or unfold comfortably and at length, as in the long, fervent, almost helter-skelter, self-unfolding sentence in which she measures out the breadth and depth of Fanny Price's love for her sailor brother William (*MP*, pp. 234–5). With her pen, Jane Austen is as dainty as a needle-worker, as purposeful as an axeman.

Let us begin with small things, because Jane Austen, like any poet worth his salt, has a passion for precision. Miss Lascelles notices the force of her 'pregnant abstractions' (of Johnsonian lineage)[6] – Miss Bates's 'desultory good will' (*E*, p. 239; cf. 'ignorant good will' in Yeats's *Easter 1916*), the basket and big bonnet that constitute for Mrs Elton the 'apparatus of happiness' (*E*, p. 358), and how Sir Walter and his two ladies step forward to greet Lady Dalrymple 'with all the eagerness compatible with anxious elegance' (*P*, p. 184). In such phrases the adjective ceases to act as a mere modifier: like a barber meditatively stroking the razor across the palm of his hand, it gives the final honing touch to the edge of humour or irony, multiple implications suddenly build up and hover over the phrase. The pregnant abstraction had its gradations. When Anne walks up to the Lodge 'in a sort of desolate tranquillity', or Mary Musgrove, at the prospect of visiting Kellynch after the Crofts have taken possession of it, is 'in a very animated, comfortable state of imaginary agitation' (*P*, pp. 36, 48), the phrases are not much more than sharply descriptive; when we read of Mrs Allen's 'busy idleness' (*NA*, p. 67), or of 'the business of love-making' that happily relieves the company of Mr Collins's presence (*P&P*, p. 129), or of the 'short parley of compliment' between Henry Crawford and Mr Yates (*MP*, p. 132) something more conspiaratorial is afoot. When Mr Collins, in the early morning, bent upon proposing (fruitlessly) to Elizabeth Bennet, escapes from Longbourn House 'with admirable slyness' (*P&P*, p. 121), the phrase resonates; and so it does (but this time with a mocking hint of a cosmic perspective) when Edmund corrects Mary's extravagant estimate of the distance they have walked – 'for he was not yet so much in love as to measure distance, or reckon time, with feminine lawlessness' (*MP*, p. 94). These short phrases, that come suddenly into view and hover for an instant like a dragonfly or a humming-bird and are gone, may stand for irrepressible flashes of humour; but they are also symptoms of strong poetic potential that hums like a fiddle-string below the surface of her apparently decorous prose. The underlying process here is true metaphor: the collision of elements none of which will give up any part of its integrity. The gift for metaphor is peculiarly the poet's gift, and cannot be learned. That it was part of Jane Austen's habit of mind can be seen in her letters, and the effect is not always funny. For example, 'Single Women have a dreadful propensity for being poor – which is one very strong argument in favour of Matrimony' (*Letters*, p. 483); she says of Mrs Cooke who is perhaps dying of an inflammation of the lungs induced by a chill taken in church that 'her mind [is] all pious composure, as may be supposed' (*Letters*, p. 245); when her brother is afflicted by the death of his wife, Jane writes to Edward Cooper, hoping that he will not send her brother 'one of his letters of cruel comfort' (*Letters*, p. 222). When she herself is about to venture the journey to Winchester to be treated for her mortal illness, she describes herself as 'a very genteel, portable sort of an Invalid' (*Letters*, p. 494).

In this, we are considering not simply a verbal locution or 'figure of speech' but a commanding process radical to poetry itself – the metaphorical process that secures and enriches the interaction not only of single words, but of elements within sentences, of sentences within paragraphs, and the collisive interaction of elements of much larger scale if they can be constructed with strong enough identity. Not only do Jane Austen's sentences adapt themselves exquisitely to their syntactical needs, but they also characteristically give the impression of shaping energy contained within deftly chosen limits – which is another indelible mark of poetic practice. On the writer's part this calls up the auditory imagination; on the reader's part it calls up, not simply an alertness to the interactions of the words themselves, but also the sense of musical phrasing. If the metaphorical process gives active substance (as it does at crucial points in Wordsworth's poems) to words that would otherwise be vague abstractions, the sense of phrasing, of musical inflection, gives body to the most minute movements of mind. Speaking in her own person, she can say of a Mr Wildman who (despite Fanny's advocacy) could see nothing in Jane's novels: 'I particularly respect him for wishing to think well of all young Ladies; it shews an amiable & a delicate Mind' (*Letters*, p. 487).

Jane Austen's impeccable sense of phrasing is a more distinctive mark of her style than her use of the isolable pregnant phrase; and she can impart this to the entirely different voice of one of her characters – for example, Mr Bennet speaking to Elizabeth:

'Next to being married, a girl likes to be crossed in love a little now and then. ... Now is your time. Here are officers enough at Meryton to disappoint all the young ladies in the country. Let Wickham be *your* man. He is a pleasant fellow, and would jilt you creditably.' (*P&P*, pp. 137–8)

She says of Mr Collins that 'The stupidity with which he was favoured by nature, must guard his courtship from any charm that could make a woman wish for its continuance' (*P&P*, p. 122); and of Mrs Allen that she was 'one of that numerous class of females, whose society can raise no other emotion than surprise at there being any men in the world who could like them well enough to marry them' (*NA*, p. 20). In these there is a hovering understatement reinforced by a sequence of double negatives actual or implied – an effect that is scarcely to be discerned in a logical analysis of the wording. When Elinor thinks of Willoughby –

She felt that his influence over her mind was heightened by circumstances which ought not in reason to have weight; by that person of uncommon attraction, that open, affectionate, and lively manner which it was no merit to possess; and by that still ardent love for Marianne, which it was not even innocent to indulge. (*S&S*, p. 333)

We catch a lighter timbre in the account of Catherine Morland –

... in many other points she came on exceedingly well; for though she could not write sonnets, she brought herself to read them; and though there seemed no chance of her throwing a whole party into raptures by a prelude on the pianoforte, of her own composition, she could listen to other people's performance with very little fatigue. (*NA*, p. 16)

The representation of Edmund's scrupulous hesitation in confronting his father with what he knows will be a pretty shaky excuse for not stopping the theatrical high jinks that he had himself disapproved of as strongly as he knew his father would – this is managed with superlative allusiveness.

Edmund's first object the next morning was to see his father alone, and give him a fair statement of the whole acting scheme, defending his own share in it as far only as he could then, in a soberer moment, feel his motives to deserve, and acknowledging with perfect ingenuousness that his concession had been attended with such partial good as to make his judgment in it very doubt-ful. (*MP*, p. 187)

As has often been noticed, a favourite device of Jane Austen's – learned no doubt from Dr Johnson – is the antithesis. Antithesis can easily pass over into metaphorical process, and for Jane Austen often does; and with meditative ease and stylistic assurance she can extend an antithesis in great variety of shape and range of complexity to give form to some of her most brilliantly constructed sentences. For example, the account of John Dashwood at the beginning of *Sense and Sensibility*.

He was not an ill-disposed young man, unless to be rather cold hearted, and rather selfish, is to be ill-disposed: but he was, in general, well respected; for he conducted himself with propriety in the discharge of his ordinary duties. Had he married a more amiable woman, he might have been made still more respectable than he was: – he might even have been made amiable himself; for he was very young when he married, and very fond of his wife. But Mrs. John Dashwood was a strong caricature of himself; – more narrow-minded and selfish. (*S&S*, p. 5)

Sometimes she will extend an antithesis (as perhaps here) to a third term, like an Alexandrine reaching out for its sixth foot; and with a playful flick at the tip of the tail turn the antithesis into an out-rageous zeugma. For example, in *Mansfield Park* –

Tom Bertram must have been thought pleasant, indeed, at any rate; he was the sort of young man to be generally liked, his agreeableness was of the kind to be oftener found agreeable than some endowments of a higher stamp, for he had easy manners, excellent spirits, a large acquaintance, and a great deal to say ... (*MP*, p. 47)

Or in the response to Mrs Churchill's death in *Emma* –

The great Mrs. Churchill was no more.

It was felt as such things must be felt. Every body had a degree of gravity and sorrow; tenderness towards the departed, solicitude for the surviving friends; and, in a reasonable time, curiosity to know where she would be buried. (*E*, p. 387)

The antithesis may be diffused, as in an aside in *Sense and Sensibility*:

Lady Middleton was equally pleased with Mrs. Dashwood. There was a kind of cold hearted selfishness on both sides, which mutually attracted them; and they sympathised with each other in an insipid propriety of demeanour, and a general want of understanding. (*S&S*, p. 229)

Elsewhere it may be infused with something like the plausible realism of Mistress Quickly's brainless inconsequence:

[Mrs Allen's] vacancy of mind and incapacity for thinking were such, that as she never talked a great deal, so she could never be entirely silent; and, therefore, while she sat at her work, if she lost her needle or broke her thread, if she heard a carriage in the street, or saw a speck upon her gown, she must observe it aloud, whether there were any one at leisure to answer her or not. (*NA*, p. 60)

The model for startling anticlimax can be seen in the juvenile 'Memoirs of Mr. Clifford':

... he was a very rich young Man & kept a great many Carriages of which I do not recollect half. I can only remember that he had a Coach, a Chariot, a Chaise, a Landeau, a Landeaulet, a Phaeton, a Gig, a Whisky, an italian Chair, a Buggy, a Curricle & a wheelbarrow. (VI, p. 43)

In its mature development, this figure can have the effect of a small land-mine, cunningly concealed, with a long-burning fuse. Of Mrs Palmer –

The openness and heartiness of her manner, more than atoned for that want of recollection and elegance, which made her often deficient in the forms of politeness; her kindness, recommended by so pretty a face, was engaging; her folly, though evident, was not disgusting, because it was not conceited; and Elinor could have forgiven every thing but her laugh. (*S&S*, p. 304)

Or of Sir Walter Elliot –

Vanity was the beginning and the end of Sir Walter Elliot's character; vanity of person and of situation. He had been remarkably handsome in his youth; and, at fifty-four, was still a very fine man. Few women could think more of their personal appearance than he did; nor could the valet of any new made lord be more delighted with the place he held in society. He considered the blessing of beauty as inferior only to the blessing of a baronetcy; and the Sir Walter Elliot, who united these gifts, was the constant object of his warmest respect and devotion. (*P*, p. 4)

By a similar process a plain gnomic statement can be suddenly shifted from the world of eternal truisms to the universe of eternal verities, achieving a sort of meditative grandeur.

Seldom, very seldom, does complete truth belong to any human disclosure; seldom can it happen that something is not a little disguised, or a little mistaken; but where, as in this case, though the conduct is mistaken, the feelings are not, it may not be very material. (*E*, p. 431)

There is a salutary reminder for us in what she said to her beloved niece Fanny Knight: 'Wisdom is better than Wit, & in the long run will certainly have the laugh on her side' (*Letters*, p. 410). It may be this recognition that imparts a tinge of elegiac sobriety to the closing paragraph of the last letter we have from Jane Austen's pen – at parting, a little smiling gesture in recognition of her love of life.

You will find Captain —— a very respectable, well-meaning man, without much manner, his wife and sister all good humour and obligingness, and I hope (since the fashion allows it) with rather longer petticoats than last year. (*Letters*, p. 498)

We cannot doubt that much of what imparts electrical vitality to Jane Austen's style was her delight in effortless virtuosity, in catching by an impossible fraction of a hair's-breadth the savour of a nuance of implication. I do not wish to venture into the discrimination of minute syntactical categories, and leave to the ingenuity of keener taxonomists than myself the following extracts from her letters.

Mr Heathcote met with a genteel little accident the other day in hunting; he got off to lead his horse over a hedge or a house or a something, & his horse in his haste trod upon his leg, or rather ancle I beleive, & it is not certain whether the small bone is not broke. (p. 85)

I hope it is true that Edward Taylor is to marry his cousin Charlotte. Those beautiful dark Eyes will then adorn another Generation at least in all their purity. (p. 87)

I give you joy of our new nephew, & hope if he ever comes to be hanged, it will not be till we are too old to care about it. (p. 272)

[Mr Blackall] was married at Clifton to a Miss Lewis, whose Father had been late of Antigua. I should very much like to know what sort of a Woman she is. He was a piece of Perfection, noisy Perfection himself which I always recollect with regard. ... I would wish Miss Lewis to be of a silent turn & rather ignorant, but naturally intelligent & wishing to learn; – fond of cold veal pies, green tea in the afternoon, & a green window blind at night. (p. 317)

Miss H[arding] is an elegant, pleasing, pretty-looking girl, about nineteen, I suppose, or nineteen and a half, or nineteen and a quarter, with flowers in her head and music at her finger ends. (p. 282)

We plan having a steady Cook, & a young giddy Housemaid, with a sedate, middle aged Man, who is to undertake the double office of Husband to the former & sweetheart to the latter. – No Children of course to be allowed on either side. (pp. 99–100)

Old Philmore was buried yesterday, & I, by way of saying something to Triggs, observed that it had been a very handsome Funeral, but his manner of reply made me suppose that it was not generally esteemed so. I can only be sure of *one* part being very handsome, Triggs himself, walking behind in his Green Coat. (pp. 488–9)

A consideration of what looked like a small figure of speech has tendrilled out to embrace most of the nervous web of Jane Austen's prose style – a style so highly charged with energy that the very restraint with which it is commanded makes us aware of a steady (though often submerged) high potential for felicity. Whatever characteristic turn of phrase we may choose, we may find variant examples of it in abundance, but not uniformly distributed either within single novels, or from novel to novel. She can call up these resources whenever occasion demands, with every gradation from plain declaration to high-spirited nonsense, from sharp irony to sombre reflection; or she can refrain from using any of them, so that the alternations from use to restraint become a principle of structure that identifies each of the novels in its own way. Her rendering of individual direct speech (with very few exceptions) is – in identity, tone, and pace – flawless. After *Sense and Sensibility* she never again tried to reproduce idiosyncratic phrasing or pronunciation as she did for the pretentious speech of the 'ignorant and illiterate' Lucy Steele; and if the failure of General Tilney turns upon Jane's failure to find his own voice for him, that too is in an early book. I admire particularly her secure handling of the arcane liturgical usage of naval persons. About her uncanny skill in discovering, without recourse to idiosyncrasy, the precise and recognisable identity of voice for each of her persons, nothing need be said: most of the admirers of Jane Austen's novels are so absorbed in her characters that they could probably, on request, produce the precise inflexion of any one of them. As though it were not enough to be able to induce her characters to speak in their own persons, she can make transitions from her own narrative to the indirect speech of her characters, or to the thought of her characters, so effortlessly that it is often difficult to decide in a particular passage whether or not it is her own comment that we are reading. Even when she does speak in her own person, as she often does, that too is usually so deftly 'placed' that it feels less like an intrusion of the omniscient author than a strain in a half-oracular counterpoint of disembodied and wise intelligence.

Another mark of her overarching poetic instinct is to be seen in her handling of detail, economically and vividly, so that actual things at times glow under her eye – a process that I have called 'naming', which, in the perceiving as in the writing, turns upon the vitality of concreteness – what Henry James admirably called 'solidity of speci-fication'. The detail of the contents of Fanny Price's east room in Mansfield Park is an outstanding instance; so too is the detail of Harriet's pathetic little love-trove in *Emma*. Jane recognised the process in actual life when Fanny Knight told her how strangely moved she was, when she went to her lover's room after he had gone away and saw there his 'dirty Shaving Rag' – Jane cried: '. . . exquisite! – Such a circumstance ought to be in print. Much too good to be lost' (*Letters*, p. 412). For she knew that simple items, told over, almost liturgically, apparently at random, can – in a novel, as in 'life' – be coloured by the consciousness of the person who names them. These items, remaining simply what they are and nothing else, can yet vibrate with an aura of implication in the very act of their being so named, so told over, so noted with solid specification. (There is a heart-rending instance of this process in James Agee's *Let Us Now Praise Famous Men* – in the catalogue of what he found in one room of the share-cropper's house after the family had gone out to work.) This is very different from 'describing' (in any accepted use of that term) as Jane shows when she criticised Anna Austen's novel: 'You describe a sweet place, but your descriptions are often more minute than will be liked. You give too many particulars of right hand & left' (*Letters*, p. 401; cf. p. 78). Describing is a matter of exhaustive delineation: naming is a matter of selective and allusive symbolising: in painting, we see the coincidence of the two perhaps in Canaletto or Vermeer.

But the process of 'naming' applies not only to objects but to the whole sub-symbolic indication of places and of the things contained within them, not simply providing a physical setting in which action can occur, but evoking obliquely from the outset the relations of persons to things, places, and other persons, and also establishing the disposition of the persons in physical space and in psychic space. For Jane Austen, the action more often than not unfolds crucially in the enclosedness of a house, a room. We could probably not draw an accurate plan of any of the houses or rooms; yet we feel sure that we could probably move about in them confidently in the dark, as persons familiar and hospitably received. Outstanding instances of the discovery of living figures in a domestic space are to be seen in *Mansfield Park*, where we hear the lovers talking quietly to each other in a room where others are present, a room large enough that they are not overheard, yet intimate enough that at any moment they may be drawn into any of the other rings of conversation that we are aware – as the lovers are – are reverberating at the same time; in the staircase encounter between Fanny and Edmund that Virginia Woolf admired; in the closing scene of *Persuasion*, the evocativeness of which could scarcely have been guessed from the first draft.

I am inclined to think that this same process of 'naming' that evocatively expands from objects to the relation of persons to objects, to a domestic space and the persons related there, applies also to the way Jane Austen draws – and draws forth – her characters: they have, at best, a 'solidity of specification' that allows them to disclose themselves as living, capable of going on surprising us, because they contain within themselves the reason why they are what they are and not otherwise. Like the objects vividly perceived, they have their own peculiar aura of presence. In the same way that we imagine that we could move about in any of Jane Austen's darkened houses, we find in our imagination that the people of her imagining grow in substance, weight, and complexity far beyond the particular limits that her economical art has assigned to them in her novels. They have the tactual solidity that can also, in the condition of poetry, be physically imprinted in words.

In *Mansfield Park*, for a time, the sisters Julia and Maria became so sundered from one another that 'there was no outward fellowship between them'; 'They were two solitary sufferers, or connected only by Fanny's consciousness' (*MP*, p. 163). The unifying force in Jane Austen's writing is the unity of her consciousness, subtle, patient, watchful, profound enough to imprint in her memory the most delicate shades of feeling, the most fugitive and ambivalent of emotions. One of Edward's younger daughters recalled how her aunt Jane 'would sit quietly working [i.e. doing needlework] beside the fire in the library, saying nothing for a good while, and then would suddenly burst out laughing, jump up and run across the room to a table where pens and paper were lying, write something down, and then come back to the fire and go on quietly working as before.' On this passage, Miss Lascelles makes this comment:

> She must have developed to a remarkable degree her faculty for living (when she chose) apart in her imagined world – and, further, for keeping the regions of that world distinct in her imagination. To be engaged at once on *Pride and Prejudice* and *Mansfield Park* – and that while still correcting the proofs of *Sense and Sensibility* – and to preserve entire the peculiar atmosphere of each – this is an achievement which shows that she could project her imagination into one or another of these fragile bubble worlds, and let it dwell there.[7]

Yet the worlds of *Mansfield Park*, *Emma*, and *Persuasion* are not bubbles; they are (like Coleridge's nightmares) foot-thick realities, though gossamer-fine. An imagined world, poetically speaking, is a world fully realised. Jane's secretiveness in securing the integrity of her imagined worlds, even from the loving solicitude of her favourite sister Cassandra, is a clear sign of the substance of those worlds: they were vulnerable, but not evanescent; not until they had found their final and proper body in words could they stand alone in our world. But the words that could be at once living and impregnable did not come to her easily or quickly. To begin with she had been sheltered by the responsive merriment she was lucky enough to find within her own populous family circle. The early novels – *Northanger Abbey, Sense and Sensibility, Pride and Prejudice* – though transformed from what they must first have been by the genius that came to her suddenly at Chawton, still rely upon the family convention, but less and less, and least of all in *Pride and Prejudice*. The ease and confidence given her as a writer by her family made her a much more daring writer than any of her contemporaries, especially her female contemporaries: she had discovered how to be lucky in writing, how to give full and risky rein to her exceptional gifts of intelligence, deep feeling, and verbal virtuosity. She found how to land on her feet like a cat, and became confident that her verbal reflexes would not betray her daring. She could say to herself, 'You are comfortable because you are under command' (*E*, p. 368).

To insist too much upon Jane Austen as a *comic* writer – even though she is often extremely funny – is to distract attention from the emotional depth and moral scope of her mature work. At times in the early novels she may be tempted into a shrewd nip of sarcastic or satrical comment; but that is not her true bent. Irony – that rarest of all gifts in a writer, a manner that nobody can fabricate – is a habit of her way of seeing, encompassing compassion and grief as well as humour. If irony, in the early novels, is often not much more than a figure of speech, in the mature novels it is the mark of Jane's steady presence behind her pen. *Le style est l'homme.* She is at once a most self-effacing writer, and – as a presence – most pervasive: an unassuming voice, a central reverberating timbre. In this, she is indeed Shakespearean, Chaucerian. For she wrote with the gravity of a born humourist, out of a life that had known its own peculiar sorrows and immedicable desolations.

As for Jane Austen's conduct of overarching drama and the interaction of plot and character, I must be content with a few general observations – because I feel that I may be sickening for a book on

Jane Austen. In this there are copious possibilities for disagreement; but Jane never hesitated to take chances, and I think we should honour her instinct. One thing, however, needs to be noted at the outset: the firm singleness of her angle of vision, imparting unquestionable authority to her omniscience; she never resorts to the comfortable convenience of the zoom-lens or the undisciplined confidence-trickery of fluid camera-movement.

In spite of the singleness and rapidity of her progress as a writer, I find in reading the novels that the first three stand in one group – *Northanger Abbey, Sense and Sensibility, Pride and Prejudice* – and *Mansfield Park, Emma*, and *Persuasion* in another. *Mansfield Park* is, I think, her great masterpiece: here all the forces are so beautifully disposed, the energy so exquisitely distributed, that even the manifestations of her poetic style (never ornate) scarcely break the surface. I shall therefore in a swift summary try to bring into focus the two poetic senses that I had distinguished at the outset.

Northanger Abbey is informed (to some extent, but not as much as we should like) by that same mode of joyous parody and exuberant burlesque that makes most of the juvenilia in Chapman's volume VI a delight to savour. She may have learned much from the prose style of Dr Johnson and the essayists, and a little from William Cowper; but in this book we meet the gift of a sunny and generous humour that, once fully assimilated into her whole tone of voice and way of seeing, was to become the hallmark of her sanity and penetration. *Northanger Abbey* is a parody of many things, but above all a parody of a certain kind of novel and of the emotional response that was expected to such novels. It is good fun in places, but the high spirits fail to establish their own centre of gravity and become (fatally, for this novel) entangled with 'life'; this makes functional demands of General Tilney that, because of the indistinctness of his nature in the early part of the book, he cannot fulfil – even though he provides one of the most astonishing reversals of expectation in the whole of Jane Austen's writing. At best *Northanger Abbey* is a sort of *Donna Quixote*, without Sancho Panza or Rosinante; and Catherine Morland is silly rather than crazy. Nevertheless, if we are searching out the quality and disposition of Jane Austen's verbal-poietic resources, this book rewards careful attention, for many of the effects lie on the surface.

Sense and Sensibility, although it may have been transformed from an original written in the burlesque manner, is her first attempt at a serious 'novel'. Witty, incisive, at times ironic, at times tender, it makes both play and capital of current expectations about a novel, and particularly about a woman's novel. The resources of a supple and disciplined prose style are here – flexible, epigrammatic if need be, capable of responding to a light touch and of moving with unpredictable swiftness. Her love of parody and a habit of self-mockery have made her a daring, as well as a cunning, navigator; she is finding how to dispose her strongest effects in understatement and obliquity, thereby not only establishing her rhetorical palette for much maturer use, but also drawing the reader from the position of observer to the quiet attentiveness of a confidante. Irony and reticence combine in an undercurrent of active intelligence and emotional precision; everything is on a small scale, the texture exquisite, the tone muted. Yet for all that can be said in praise of detail and effects, the mastery is not yet assured. There are thin passages, places where inner tension flags and we find ourselves reading – at times (near the end) – out of respect rather than delight. The drawing of Marianne is perhaps tinged more with satire than with irony, the theme is more parabolic than the action can take in its stride, the story an expanded version of antithesis with the elements drawn to life size. She seems to have a point to make, not so much about society as about the relation between art and life. *Sense and Sensibility* is not usually regarded as a defective novel; yet it does, in ways difficult to define, fall short of self-sustaining perfection. It may be a question of her difficulty of combining at one stroke a variety of talents already highly developed. For all the signs of her genius are present: exhilaration, subtlety of effect, confident delight in the exercise of powers greater than the book calls for, the composure that goes with a knowledge deeper and more comprehensive than is allowed to appear on the surface, a habit of reticence that is much less a figurative device than the ironic exercise of intellectual good manners.

Pride and Prejudice opens *con brio*, with a crackling dramatic *panache* that *Sense and Sensibility* had not prepared us for. Even though the manuscript original of this book is earlier than the original of *Sense and Sensibility*, the book declares, from the very outset, a higher order of accomplishment and assurance. In every way, the advance of *Pride and Prejudice* is impressive, especially in the drawing of the complementary persons of Jane and Elizabeth. If at first Darcy seems, as a gruffer version of that fool Collins, unassimilable to the emotional probabilities of the story, he is in the end satisfactorily transformed into a man worthy to receive Elizabeth's hand; and Jane and Elizabeth are drawn with a depth that prevents the book from settling into the fable-with-a-moral that the title tempts us to expect. The only sign of uncertainty is in her failure to master what practically every novelist that came after her also failed to master – the self-conscious and disturbing awareness that she was writing a *novel*, that certain things were expected of a novel and of its story; even if she were to refrain from doing what was expected, she could not escape that expectation. Rewritten at a single impulse from the version that Cadell had rejected fifteen years earlier, *Pride and Prejudice* is justly esteemed among the small handful of best English novels. Distracted, it may be, by a certain publicity of intent, it is too deceptively effortless to encourage imitation, and is much too adult to be recommended to school-children. If Jane Austen had stopped writing there, she would be seen to have triumphed. But she could do even better than that; and did so, at once, in *Mansfield Park*.

To enjoy *Pride and Prejudice* we accept on trust certain moral conventions with ironic reservation, and with amused detachment observe a microtome slice of the *comédie humaine* so thin that – perhaps because of its very thinness – speaks for a central issue in life, marriage and money; we are allowed to entertain the possibility that the mark of parochial barbarism would be to pretend that the issue of marriage and money is a trivial one. In *Mansfield Park* something rather more compelling happens. Whether or not we accept the conventions, and whether or not we 'identify' with any of the persons in the story, is – as with most fully realised works of art – curiously irrelevant. We are drawn into an action of ineluctable internal power and logic, self-determinate, self-consistent; an action at once simple and complex which, without ever losing its way or checking its momentum, is held in an exquisite balance of composed forces, like the slow movement of a posthumous quartet. A finely articulated universe of feeling and implication grows out of the roots of the life peculiar to it, and reflects back upon life with a strong and penetrating light. There are stylistic and managerial similarities with the novels that came before, and with the two that were to follow; but *Mansfield Park* stands apart as different in kind, ordered from within as none of the others is. The clear identity of each volume gives the book exceptional interior strength and vitality. I have difficulty in reading it as a comedy. How she came upon this universe, constructed it, and sustained it, we cannot say; it should not have been possible – or at least no more possible than to trace out the figure of tragedy itself. The book seems to have depended upon a very fragile imaginative poise; when she turned at once to write *Emma* she had lost it.

Jane Austen, like Milton, did not like to repeat herself; after each novel she moved forward to venture something that she had not attempted before. Much of the actual writing of *Emma* is, in detail, apparently more accomplished and of deeper implication than the general run of *Mansfield Park*: she explores, as she had not dared earlier, the intricate and paradoxical inner goings-on of a woman in love; from her love of symmetry, of correspondence and anti-thesis, of converging and diverging movements, she evolves a pattern almost geometrical in its disposition of internal forces; and with unruffled forthrightness she presents a group of people who from their first utterances give omen of the persons we are to find them to be. Yet the book as a whole is comparatively static, and I do not find Emma's threefold self-imposed ordeal of self-discovery enough of a moral escalation to make the book – as with protective zeal we might have hoped – a sort of *Emma Agonistes*. The luminous integration has gone slightly adrift; not breaking into disorder (for she was incapable of that), but to the subtle undermining of the total dramatic effect that can bring probability and necessity into one identity. Though there is more striking incident in this book than in anything earlier, *Emma* is deficient in commanding action, and feels like a fiction in a way that only *Northanger Abbey* does. Her sheer love of exercising her powers of dramatic invention even leads her at times into slight over-indulgence: some speeches of Miss Bates, though unsurpassed in autonomous vivacity, dislocate the swift apperception of the position Miss Austen has adopted, and interrupt 'the wonderful velocity of thought'. *Emma* is much admired, and rightly so; yet the closing chapter is the one place in all her novels where I feel that she is writing a little perfunctorily, with less respect for her reader than is her use; as though it could be said for the author, rather than for the actors, that all passion is spent.

Persuasion, in its smaller mass, is – like *Emma* – comparatively static, a study rather than a drama. The book was probably intended to be as it is; it is, of its kind, very fine, and is more trenchantly human than *Emma*. A dark emotional tone enfolds the central person (despite her vividness) and spreads through every incident and even into the landscape that Jane Austen is alleged to be insensitive to. The darkness feels as though it sprang from some deep personal source, an acute awareness of how some casual incident or circumstance – that nobody could have recognised as crucial and that could have been rescued only by exceptional vigilance or by grace – can prove to be a sorrowful, even irreversible, turning-point in a life; how in life (as Rilke says of art) there are no classes for beginners. Anne's strength and sombre patience is surely Jane's; and if the reversal of Captain Wentworth's regard seems artificially delayed for the purposes of the plot, and Mrs Smith's privileged information is so complete and accessible as to make her seem a very mundane *dea ex machina*, we can accept all that in gratitude for the disclosure of a heart and mind that we had often caught glimpses of in novels more high-spirited and apparently more superficial. In testing the veracity of our own perception we may say that for Jane Austen the turning-point in the history of *her* heart came about, not through misunderstanding or through accident of occasion, but through death. The darkness may come from life; but the mastery of a pervasive emotional tension flowing (in the novel) from a single experiencing centre, is itself a poetic achievement brought about through command of tonal consistency and the craftsmanship of a spare and finely modulated score. If Jane Austen can be seen as Mozartian, it is in her character that *Persuasion* should be her Clarinet Quintet.

Nothing would be more agreeable than to savour the details of *Mansfield Park*. But I must use despatch and can notice only in general terms some of the poetical features that strike me as essential to the unassuming but masterly conduct of this book. The opening chapter is forthright, abrupt, with an occasional asperity of tone that had not been heard even in *Pride and Prejudice*; it is stylised, urgent, without agreeable obliquity, setting the situation as swiftly and emphatically as possible. The opening is not much less formalised and impatient than the opening of *King Lear*; what is to happen must be seen at once to need to happen according to inner necessity. And when we come to the end, the book closes with corresponding despatch, yet with something of the elegiac recognition of sheer necessity, not fading back into life but rounding this universe of her imagining to a close without regret. 'I only intreat every body to believe that exactly at the time when it was quite natural that it should be so, and not a week earlier, Edmund did cease to care about Miss Crawford, and became as anxious to marry Fanny, as Fanny herself could desire' (p. 470). Within the boundaries of the abrupt opening and closing of the story, Jane Austen moves with consummate ease so that for the most part we cannot tell the dancer from the dance. All those problems of technique, in securing both

the autonomy of characters and the vocal omniscience of the author
– problems that seem to have filled the hearts of other novelists with
dismay or turned them at times to grotesque extremes of ingenuity –
she manages them all (as Virginia Woolf said with an entirely
different import) with 'the swift composure of a fish'. For example,
she can, without preparation, begin a monologue which is answered
by a second speaker; and gradually we are aware of others present,
and of the place, and the disposition of emotional forces at play
there, and a whole complex tissue of relations unfolds. This is a feat
that I had been led to suppose was Henry James's unique preroga-
tive. Again, the strict constraints that she interposes to shape the
energy of invention impart momentous dramatic weight with small
effort. When, after the collapse of the *Lovers' Vows*, Henry Crawford
tells his sister that 'My plan is to make Fanny Price in love with
me. . . . I cannot be satisfied without Fanny Price, without making a
small hole in Fanny Price's heart' (p. 229) the effect is as shocking as
if he were announcing a plan for cold-blooded rape.

I must not multiply examples. I wish to add only that in the poetic
conduct of her language in *Mansfield Park*, and in her realising of
a stylised plot in probable action, I am reminded of the uncon-
strained lyrical force of Cézanne's painting, in which naturalistic
fidelity, a profound sense of underlying physical structure, and a
purely abstract rendering of colour, mass, and space combine in the
felicity of an axiom. And in *Mansfield Park* I am often reminded too
of Bartók's *Music for Strings, Percussion, and Celeste*, constructed
as it is upon one nerveless little five-note tune: spare, brilliant, inventive, eloquent.

But there is one other suggestion I have to make. It is universally
accepted that Jane Austen is a 'comic' writer: she makes us laugh;
she traces out (it is said) the foibles, follies, and self-deceptions of a
society strictly limited in locale and class. The standard scheme for
comedy, however, whether on the stage or in a novel, is that it places
more or less unchanging figures against a variable and changing
social background. And Jane Austen's novels (though they are not
all the same) do not match that scheme. In them, the people change
within the confines of inflexible social convention, moral prescript,
and amatory mechanism; they have an acute, almost obsessive,
internality; they are enclosed and confined. Edwin Muir (in the
chapter from which I have already quoted) said that 'the dramatic
novel need not be tragic, and the first novelist who practised it with
consummate success in England – Jane Austen – consistently

avoided and probably was quite incapable of sounding the tragic note.'[8] I wonder, however, whether we are correct in identifying 'the tragic note' as necessarily dark, disastrous, desolating. Is there no other way of bringing a sense of pity-and-fear to a state of exaltation – the pleasure peculiar to tragedy? Aristotle tells us that there were tragedies that had a prosperous outcome – by which I take it that he did not mean 'dark' tragedies with a happy ending, because for Aristotle the end is always implicit in the beginning. He evidently knew such tragedies, but none has come to us among the few survivors from the Greek theatre. Aristotle, with his intense concentration on the peculiar configuration of the tragic action and the integrity of it – the single figure the whole play traces – recognised that there were works that traced the specific arc of tragic action under the guidance of stories or plots that were not intrinsically disastrous. Is it possible that Jane Austen may have achieved such a feat; not in all her books, to be sure, but in *Mansfield Park*?

I began by declaring my wonder at an achievement in language so marvellous that no term more trifling than 'poetry' could hope to encompass it. I have also hinted that in the dramatic conduct of her novels there may still be depths to be plumbed. Happy the critic of Jane Austen. She has given us plenty to think about, but, with impeccable decorum, she confronts us, not with problems and puzzles, but with marvels; her art is never importunate. If my praise seems excessive, I can reply only with the disclaimer she gave to a man whose coarse pomposity amused and disgusted her: 'I must make use of this opportunity to thank you, dear Sir, for the very high praise you bestow on my ... novels. I am too vain to wish to convince you that you have praised them beyond their merits' (*Letters*, p. 442). And if we ask how she did it, the reply seems to be given in *Emma*: 'What did she say? – Just what she ought, of course. A lady always does.'

NOTES

1 *Jane Austen: the Critical Heritage*, ed. B. C. Southam (London, 1968) pp. 127, 130.

2 *Jane Austen and her Art* (Oxford, 1939) p. 106.

3 Southam, pp. 87–105; 122–3; 148–66.

4 Southam, pp. 130, 243, 157, 243.

5 *The Structure of the Novel* (London, 1928) pp. 42–6.

6 Lascelles, p. 109.

7 Lascelles, pp. 32–3.

8 Muir, p. 42.

Index

The entry for Jane Austen has been reserved for references to her life, to general comments on her art, and to minor works and the non-fiction. Discussions of the major works are indexed separately under their titles, and there are also separate entries for characters and places in the novels that receive more than passing attention. References to works by other authors are indexed under the authors' names. Italicised page numbers refer to major discussions.